Here Comes The Drama

A Ferris & Sloan Story

Christa Innis

Copyright © 2025 by Christa Innis

All rights reserved.

No part of this book may be reproduced, stored in a retrieval system, or transmitted in any form or by any means, electronic, mechanical, photocopying, recording, or otherwise, without the prior written permission of the publisher, except for the use of brief quotations in a review.

ISBN: 979-8-9985754-0-2 (Print)
ISBN: 979-8-9985754-1-9 (eBook)

Cover design by Oak&Air Creative Agency

Developmental editing and literary representation by Jessica Berg, Rosecliff Literary

Copyediting and proofreading by Hannah Flood

Published by Eleanora Press

Disclaimer:

This is a work of fiction. Names, characters, places, and events are either products of the author's imagination or are used fictitiously. Any resemblance to actual persons, living or dead, real events, or existing fictional characters is purely coincidental. The characters Ferris and Sloan are original creations and are not affiliated with or inspired by any existing media or franchise.

Printed in the United States of America

To my amazing husband, Zach—your unwavering love and support make everything feel possible. You are my rock, and I couldn't have done this without you.

To my beautiful daughter—you inspire me every day to be better. You are my driving force, and I hope you always have the courage to chase your own dreams.

And to all my incredible fans and followers—thank you for embracing the silly skits I shared on social media and for allowing me the space to be vulnerable and create. Through your encouragement, I've rediscovered a part of myself I thought I'd lost, and for that, I will be forever grateful.

Part 1

Chapter 1

Kate can't believe her ears. She picks up her glass of wine, throws back what's left, then stands up and storms out of the living room with a loud huff.

Her daughter, Jenny, watches her leave in pure confusion, then glances at everyone else before quickly jumping off the couch to follow her. "Mom, are you okay?" she yells after her, hurrying closer. She notices a drop of red wine has stained her mom's white blouse.

"Ugh! I just know she's doing this to get my son away from me," Kate charges into the next room looking unsteady, like she's about to burst.

"What are you talking about?" Jenny quickly interjects. "Sloan isn't taking anyone away from you." Her eyes drift toward the window, where snow has just started falling. At first, it was light and quiet—barely noticeable. But now, it's beginning to fall in thick clumps, sticking to the glass like something trying to get in.

Kate pushes up her round brown glasses as a bead of sweat drips from her forehead. "Did you not just hear them? They come waltzing in here on Thanksgiving to tell us they're not going to be here on Christmas!" Her voice trembles with a mix of hurt and disbelief. For a moment, she questions whether or not she's overreacting—but the thought vanishes as quickly as it came. Her stance is firm now. There's no going back.

Jenny looks at her mother, dumbfounded. She takes a deep breath to save herself from calling out her mother's ridiculousness right here, right now. "Yeah, they planned a vacation together. I think that's perfectly acceptable." She runs a hand through her long dirty blonde hair, exhaling sharply. "You can't tell them to not go on vacation together."

The snow was falling harder now, piling on the windowsill in soft, heavy heaps—like the weight of everything left unsaid in the room.

"But on Christmas? There are three hundred and sixty-four other days of the year! Why'd they have to pick Christmas?" Kate's voice gets louder each time she talks and there is clear panic in her voice, like she's been robbed.

"My guess is because they wanted to spend the holidays together," Jenny sarcastically replies. "This isn't some weird thing for a boyfriend to do with his girlfriend."

Kate rolls her eyes before putting her head down in her hands and mumbling, "You just watch, Jenny. This is how it all starts, then soon they're just not going to show up for certain holidays." She looks up, staring off as if she just had an epiphany hearing her own words.

"Mom, you should be happy that Ferris found someone he loves and wants to spend his time with," Jenny says, resting a hand on her mom's back. "Now, can we go back out there, put on a happy face, and enjoy the rest of Thanksgiving?" She raises both pointer fingers to the corners of her mouth, exaggerating a smile.

After a long pause, Kate pulls a tissue out of her pocket and dabs her face, although Jenny didn't see any tears. "Fine," Kate stands tall, touches up her short brown hair, and forces a painful, wide smile. "How's this?"

"Great," Jenny gives her a swift thumbs up and gestures for her mother to follow her back out into the living room where the others are.

Jenny is the first to step back into her parents' living room, where she spots her brother, Ferris, at the fridge, grabbing two beers—one for their dad, Ted, and one for himself. The room is warm with the scent of Thanksgiving leftovers, and the muffled hum of conversation drifts in from the dining room.

"You need more wine, babe?" Ferris calls out over his shoulder, his voice casual but affectionate. His short, faintly golden hair with brown undertones is slightly tousled, a few strands falling in his face as he reaches for the fridge.

Sloan is curled up on the couch, legs crossed, swirling the last bit of red wine in her glass. Her long, almost-black hair drapes over one shoulder, catching the warm glow of the Christmas lights.

She's wearing a soft knit sweater dress in a deep burgundy, paired with thick socks—comfortable, yet casually stylish in a way that always seemed natural to her. She looks over at him with a small, knowing smile.

"No, I still have some left, thanks," Sloan smirks and turns just as she notices Jenny walking back in. "Oh, hey! Everything okay?" Her eyes flick between Jenny and Kate, searching for any sign of what just happened. She knew Kate was upset about the trip, but sometimes, it was easier to pretend she didn't notice than to invite more drama.

"Yeah, sorry about that," Jenny says quickly. "My mom thought she ate something bad." Her voice is light, but there's a flicker of something else beneath it. Before Sloan can press, Jenny shifts gears. "So, anyway! Tell us more about your trip. Where are you guys going?" She walks right up to Sloan and sits down at the chair across from her.

Kate reenters the room, lingering near the doorway, arms crossed, displeasure practically radiating off her.

"We're going to Santa Monica," Sloan replies quietly, combing her hair behind her ear. "I've never been before. Ferris knows I hate the snow, so he planned for a warm vacation to get us out of here. It was all his idea, so he'll have more of the details." She looks over at Ferris, now seated next to her on the couch.

Ferris hands a beer to his dad, then takes a sip of his own and leans back. "Yeah, I mean I don't have too much planned yet, but I thought we'd escape the dreaded Milwaukee winter and soak up some sun for once." He nods toward the window, where thick clumps of snow swirl in the wind, before reaching over and gently taking Sloan's hand.

Sloan glances down at their intertwined fingers, a soft smile forming as warmth blooms in her chest. But even in the comfort of this moment, she can feel Kate's disapproval lingering like a heavy cloud that refuses to pass.

"That sounds amazing!" Jenny jumps in quickly. "What do you think, Mom? Doesn't that sound fun?" Her voice is too chipper, eyes flicking toward Kate with the hope that a simple question might smooth over the crack in the room.

Ted shifts slightly in his chair, his gaze fixed on his wife. He raises his eyebrows just enough to signal *go easy, try to be happy*. But it's clear he's bracing himself. After almost thirty years of marriage, he knows her moods, her tells—he knows exactly where this could be headed.

When Kate answers, "Yeah, it sounds great," with a snap of sarcasm, Ted exhales—just barely. For a split second, it seems like that might be the end of it. But then, he catches the sudden shift in her expression. She gasps. His shoulders stiffen. Here it comes.

"Maybe we should all go!" Her somber mood instantly flips to excitement, making her way to the front of the room.

Sloan tenses. Every instinct screams at her to shut the idea down, but she hesitates. It's not her place. Kate has always been dismissive of her—why would this moment be any different?

"Funny, Mom," Ferris cuts in, forcing a chuckle, but there's an edge of unease in his voice.

"No, I'm serious! Wouldn't it be great?" Kate stands as if she's launching into a full-blown presentation. She turns to her husband, eyes bright with enthusiasm. "Ted, shouldn't we go?"

Ted takes a deep breath. "Kate, we can go to Santa Monica any other time. I don't think we need to hijack our son's vacation with his girlfriend." He runs a hand across his forehead as if trying to smooth out the wrinkles he's certain are forming.

"Oh, come on! It'll be so much fun to spend Christmas together in California." Kate is starting to act like this is the best idea she's ever had. She turns back towards Ferris, gesturing to the Christmas tree already up in the living room, decorated with ornaments with brief reminders of their childhood. "You know how much Christmas means to me."

Ferris opens his mouth like he's about to say something when a defeated look appears on his face and he stops. He knows his mom. She doesn't take hearing "no" very well and it would turn into a huge ordeal if he tries to push back now. He tries to figure out a way to get her to back off a bit and decides to change the subject, leaning forward and peeking around Sloan to catch his dad's eye. "Wow, Dad, I am so full. That turkey you made was fantastic—way better than last year's."

Ted beams, about to respond when Kate jumps in. "It was! You really know how to make the holidays special around here... all of you." Her smile is a little too bright as she claps her hands together. "Now, who wants dessert?!" she asks, already pivoting toward the kitchen.

"That sounds great, I'll help you," Jenny says as she shakes her head behind her mom in disappointment.

As Kate and Jenny disappear into the kitchen, Ted leans in, lowering his voice for only Ferris and Sloan to hear. "Hey," he says, offering a warm smile, "I think the trip sounds perfect. You two deserve it." He pauses, his eyes flicking toward the kitchen. "And you know how your mother is—she just needs a minute to adjust. Don't let it ruin your plans."

Ferris puts his arm around Sloan, gently pulling her closer. There was no doubt in his mind—Sloan didn't want his mom on their couple's vacation, and he wasn't going to let it happen. It wasn't unusual for his mom to try to control new situations. In the past, he might've let it slide, but not this time. Sloan was different. She was his person.

She was articulate, compassionate, and beautiful—but not in a way that begged for attention, more like the kind of beauty that you noticed slowly, then couldn't unsee.

Ferris used to tell his mom everything. Back when he was a kid, it had felt natural—easy, even. She always knew what to say, always had a plan. But then he remembered the summer after seventh grade.

He had been obsessed with skateboarding, saving up every dollar from mowing lawns to buy his first board. He and his best friend, Ben, would spend hours practicing tricks, wiping out on the pavement, laughing at their bruises. Until Kate decided it was dangerous.

"He's a bad influence," she had told him one night, arms crossed, lips pressed into a thin line. "Always pushing you to do reckless things. You'll break an arm, Ferris. And what about school? You need to focus."

He had argued—of course he had. But then came the nagging, the disappointed sighs, the gentle but firm reminders of all the things she had done for him. "I'm only trying to protect you."

And so, he quit. He told Ben he was too busy and that his mom needed his help around the house. It wasn't true, but it was easier than fighting about it or living with guilt.

Now, years later, Ferris knew better. He saw the pattern, the way she packaged control as concern. It wasn't just about skateboarding, or friends, or even his career—it was everything. Every choice. Every step he took.

Which is why he barely told her anything anymore.

They enjoy their dessert together, moving past the idea of them all going to Santa Monica for Christmas. Ferris did his best to get his mom talking about her new book club with the neighbor ladies. After dessert, he and Sloan start inching their way to the door, getting on their shoes and coats so they can head home.

"Oh! Leaving so soon?!" Kate's voice carries a hint of surprise, though it's clear she's more focused on keeping them there than acknowledging how difficult she could be.

Sloan turns and smiles at Kate, trying to keep things light. "Yeah, it's getting late. I'm hoping to call my mom on the way home since we didn't get to see her this year for Thanksgiving."

Kate ignores Sloan's comment and turns towards Ferris, "Well, bye guys, it was so great having you guys here for Thanksgiving, as you should be for all holidays," Kate accentuates the "all" to make sure they remember where she stands.

Ferris forces a smile before placing his hand on Sloan's back as they turn to leave. "I'll meet you in the car in just a sec. I forgot to grab some pie to take home."

"Oh, yeah, sure. Bye, Kate. Bye, Ted. Thanks again for having us—the food was delicious," Sloan says, wrapping her scarf around her neck as she steps out of the house.

"Okay, so there's Pumpkin and Apple Pie left, which did you want? You know what? I'll go grab you some of each," Kate says as she hurries into the kitchen.

"Uh, I'll have some apple, but actually, I don't really need any pie," Ferris says, checking to make sure Sloan hasn't walked back into the house. He looks directly at his mom. "Can I talk to you for a second?"

"Sure, of course. Look, I'm really excited for this vacation. I'm going to start planning tonight!" Kate interrupts, a little too quickly. Ted, easing his way back into the living room, props his legs up in the recliner. His eyes are tired, and it's clear he's had enough for the night. He knows exactly how his wife can be, so he shuts down, retreating into his own space.

"No, Mom. You can't come," Ferris says, his tone firmer this time.

"What do you mean? Why? Oh wait, you're breaking up with Sloan, aren't you? I knew something was off tonight."

"What? No... nothing was off with us tonight. I'd really like this trip to be just Sloan and me, so we can have some alone time."

"Alone time?!" Kate scoffs. "What do you need alone time for? You already live together! I hardly see you anymore." She pauses before adding, "I wouldn't want to intrude, but maybe I could just stay nearby. Dad and I will get our own hotel room, we'll have our own time—but we can meet up for dinners and stuff." She continues rummaging through the kitchen cabinets, searching for a container big enough for the leftover pie.

"No. I'm sorry. I love you, but this trip is for Sloan and me. I need you to respect that." Ferris states.

For a moment, Kate wonders if she's being too harsh, if maybe she's giving him a reason to pull away. But the thought is fleeting—she quickly reminds herself of everything she's done for him over the years. He still needs her.

"Well, what if something happens? I could help you plan it!"

"It's already planned and paid for." Ferris exhales. "But look, I need to tell you why it just needs to be the two of us."

"Okay," Kate stops what she's doing and stands there, wide-eyed, staring at her son.

"Actually, I kind of want to tell Dad too really quickly. Hey, Dad, can you come in here?"

Ted hurries over from the other room to join them.

"So really quick, I wanted to talk to you and Mom to let you know why I want to take Sloan on vacation, just the two of us."

"Oh man, I think I know where this is going," Ted says with a big smile on his face.

Ferris looks over at his mom, who looks like she's just seen a ghost.

"I actually plan on surprising Sloan and proposing the first night we're there." The room goes silent, and Ferris looks at both of his parents for any kind of approval. Ted looks at Kate, waiting for her reaction.

"Proposing what?" she responds slowly, her voice tinged with uncertainty as she tries to piece it all together. She knew exactly what he meant, but if he saw how confused she was maybe he would take it as a sign that the timing wasn't right.

"Come on, Kate," Ted finally jumps in. "Oh my gosh, Ferris, this is so exciting." He walks up and wraps his arms around his son, giving him a strong, reassuring pat on the back, the silent gesture filled with unspoken congratulations.

Kate just stands there staring at the two of them, vowing her naivety.

"Marriage, mom," Ferris says as he loosens his dad's grip on him and turns, "What else am I going to propose?"

"What? But you hardly know her! Are you sure she's the right one for you?" she starts shuffling around the kitchen, cleaning up items from dinner, forgetting about the pie completely. Ted is caught in the middle, looking around like he's praying for an out.

"I don't consider two and a half years together 'hardly knowing each other'. Yes, I know she's the right one for me," Ferris's voice is tight as he peers out the window behind him to make sure Sloan is okay in the car.

His mom isn't backing down. "But you're so young. Maybe just give it some more time..."

Ted can't hold his tongue anymore, "I think what your mom is trying to say is congratulations. Right, Kate?" He says, looking over at her, giving her every opportunity to change her tune.

"Congratulations? It hasn't even happened yet! He's just telling us his hypothetical plan. He still has to really think about it," she smiles. "I don't think you realize how big of a decision this truly is, Ferris." She says condescendingly, putting her hand on the counter to reach out and touch his.

Ferris pulls his hand back and moves away from the counter. "Okay, well, I can see where this conversation is going." He takes a moment to take a breath and gather himself, "Thank you, Dad, for the congratulations. Sloan's waiting in the car, so I gotta get going. But, um, thanks, I guess?"

He hurries past his parents and out the door before he realizes he forgot the pie. "Shit."

Chapter 2

The next morning, Ferris rubs the sleep from his eyes as he walks quietly down the hallway, with early morning light spilling through the curtains. The house was quiet except for the faint hum of the heater kicking on. As he turns the corner into the living room, he spots her—Sloan—curled up on the couch in one of his hoodies, cradling a mug of coffee between both hands.

She looks peaceful, but there's something in her eyes. Distant. Thoughtful. The kind of quiet that wasn't restful.

"Couldn't sleep?" Ferris asks gently, his voice still thick with sleep.

Sloan looks up and offers a soft smile. "Too much spinning in my brain."

He crosses the room and drops onto the couch beside her, slipping his arm behind her shoulders. She leans into him without a word. They sit like that for a moment—quiet and connected.

"You okay?"

"I'm good. Just... thinking about yesterday. How quickly things turned. Will your mom ever like me?"

Ferris sighs and rests his chin on her shoulder. "She likes you! She just runs on emotion. The thought of losing control scares her," he said quietly.

Sloan leans back, putting some space between them. "Losing control? She's unraveling because you want to take me on a trip?" She takes a slow sip of her coffee, eyes narrowing. "I've never felt so *overlooked* by someone in my life."

"I know," Ferris says, his voice soft. "But it used to be worse."

Sloan's eyebrows shoot up. "Worse? We've been together for over two years, Ferris. It's only escalated. I don't know how much more I can take." She turns her head, gaze drifting to the window. The morning light outlines her silhouette, but there's nothing soft about the distance in her voice. Outside, the snow from yesterday's storm clings to the branches of the trees, the white flakes still heavy and pristine, untouched by the wind. It felt like the calm before the storm—a quiet, but palpable tension.

Ferris reaches for her hand, holding it tightly. "Sloan, I need you to hear me—I choose you. I won't let this keep happening."

He meant it. Every word. But somewhere deep inside, a familiar fear flickers—one that whispers he'd be seen as ungrateful, disloyal even, for standing up to the woman who raised him.

It was wild to think how far they'd come. Ferris remembered the first night they met—both dragged to a mutual friend's party they hadn't even wanted to attend.

When he walked in, he spotted the most beautiful girl in the back of the room. She was far away, but her smile lit up everyone around her. He knew right then he had to talk to her.

So, he went for it.

"Hey! There you are—how have you been?" he said, pretending they were old friends reuniting.

Sloan blinked, her brows knitting together. "Uh... hey?"

Ferris scrambled, throwing out vague mentions of "mutual friends" and "that thing a while back." He could tell she didn't buy a word of it—but instead of calling him out, she tilted her head, clearly amused.

"You're full of it," she said, lips twitching into a smirk.

"Completely."

And somehow, that was all it took. They talked for hours, laughing and falling into an easy rhythm—the kind that made it feel like they'd known each other forever. She told him about how she was in school for teaching, how she wanted to mold minds and make kids feel seen. The way her eyes lit up when she talked about it made it impossible not to be drawn in.

At one point, Ferris leaned back, grinning. "So, what's your name?"

"Sloan."

Ferris laughed. "You've gotta be kidding me."

She raised an eyebrow. "What?"

"I'm Ferris." He paused, waiting for it to click. "You know... the 80s cult classic?"

Sloan blinked, then laughed. "Oh! Yeah—but Sloan is actually my grandmother's maiden name."

Ferris chuckled. "Still. That's too perfect."

"Fate?" she teased.

"Definitely fate."

And now, here they were—navigating chaos, holding on through the storm.

***

The smell of coffee fills the air as Jenny waits in line at the local coffee shop. She breathes in deeply, needing the aroma to help her go into this conversation with a clear head. There was always something so relaxing about being in a coffee shop, but especially this one, her favorite. It's where she comes when she needs to finish up her papers for school.

"Hi there, I'll have one medium vanilla latte with almond milk and one medium plain black coffee." She taps her card to pay and walks to the pick-up area.

As she waits, she gets a text from Ferris: *How's it going with mom?*

She quickly texts back that she's meeting with her now and will update him soon. Ferris had called her last night to share his plans for proposing to Sloan. Sensing the stress in his voice, Jenny immediately offered to take their mom out and make it clear she wasn't invited on the trip and that her input wasn't needed.

"Jenny?" The barista from behind the counter calls out as Jenny walks up to grab it. She smiles big, with a gentle, "Thank you," before adding a couple bucks to their tip jar. She turns around to look for where her mom managed to find a table.

"Jenny! Over here," Kate waves her hands profusely and starts to stand up.

As Jenny makes her way over, she thinks of how this conversation might go. Picturing everything from her mom finally understanding to getting up quickly and storming out.

"So hunny, what did you want to chat about? How is everything going at work?"

"Everything is fine with work, just busy as usual," Jenny says, looking down at the small arrow tattoo on her wrist, reminding her to always move forward. Jenny works as a bartender at a brewery in town while finishing up her degree in Psychology. She loves it, but has a hard time separating her work from everything else.

"That's great! You know, being busy is good," Kate wraps her hands around her coffee cup. "Well, I'm hoping you can get a good break around Christmas so we can all enjoy our time in California, and you won't have to worry about schoolwork the whole time." She picks up her coffee to take a sip.

"I do get a break around Christmas, but actually, that was what I wanted to talk to you about. Mom, you cannot just show up to Ferris's proposal."

"Jenny, I'm not gonna just show up, but if we're already in Santa Monica, I don't see why he wouldn't want us there."

Jenny crosses her arms, her jaw tightening as she fixes her mother with a hard stare. "I don't want to hear any more excuses. He already told you he just wanted it to be the two of them and no one else there."

Kate pouts, "Well, it's not like he owns Santa Monica. It's simply impossible to block someone from visiting another city."

Jenny cannot take this. "Right, but don't you think they deserve this special moment?" Of course, her mom *doesn't* think they deserve a special moment. It's not special if *she's* not there. Convincing her mom was going to prove much harder than she thought.

"Look honey, they don't even know what they want." Of this, Kate was sure. They were only 27 and 28, practically children. She would help guide them through this stage of their lives and if in a few more years they wanted to get married, then, and only then, she would support it. But from the looks of it, Sloan was not ready for marriage. She obviously just wanted Ferris for his good looks and money, and Sloan needed to be reminded that Ferris was her son first.

"Mom, how can you say that? He's not a little kid. They've been dating for a few years," Jenny strokes her forehead. Even though Ferris was her younger brother, he had always been more mature than her, although she would never admit this out loud. They hadn't always gotten along, but she felt protective of him, especially when it came to their mother.

"Maybe if I just called and talked to Sloan, I could give her my input about getting married so young. I just think she wants a flashy ring. She doesn't understand that a proposal and a ring also mean lifelong commitment," her voice gets eerily calmer.

Jenny slams her coffee cup on the table. "No, no, *no*. You cannot call and talk to her. She has no clue this is happening. Plus, I think she has her own mother to give her unsolicited life advice."

"Jenny, we're in a public place, you need to calm yourself down." Kate looks around quickly to make sure no one is watching them, but it's too late. "You're not gonna like this, but I actually already started looking at rentals," Kate opens up her purse, pulls out her phone, and after a few seconds of scrolling, hands it to Jenny. "Look at this one!"

"No, Mom, you can't do this," her voice was a mix of disbelief and frustration.

"Oh, Jenny, you're being so dramatic! Years from now you're gonna look back on this and laugh. We're all gonna be there and have amazing pictures from this great family vacation. Now, I'm gonna call Ferris." Before Jenny can say anything, she picks up her phone.

"That's weird," Kate looks at her phone as if it's broken, "it went right to voicemail."

MEANWHILE...

"I cannot believe you moved our trip up three weeks!" Sloan says to Ferris as the cab pulls up to the airport drop-off.

Ferris looks over at her and smiles. God, she's so beautiful. "Maybe this is what I had planned all along. But I guess you'll never know." He winks as he shuffles out of the car, grabbing their luggage to head in.

***

"Ladies and gentlemen, welcome to Los Angeles. The local time is 3:45 PM, and the weather is a pleasant 75 degrees with clear skies. We appreciate you choosing to fly with us today. On behalf of the entire crew, we wish you a wonderful stay here in the Los Angeles area or wherever your travels may take you."

Sloan slowly opens her eyes and looks out the window, her head resting on Ferris's shoulder. "Wow, are we there already? That flight went so fast."

Ferris looks down at her and kisses her forehead. "Yeah, that happens when you pass out the whole way there," he laughs. Sloan sits up to grab a hair tie from her bag and throws her hair up into a messy bun.

About 30 minutes go by when they finally start to line up to get off the plane. As they walk off the plane an older woman from behind calls out after them, "Excuse me? I think you dropped this!"

Sloan turns around to see the woman holding out her green sweater. "Oh my! Thank you so much!" she says as she takes it. As she starts to turn back, the lady continues to talk.

"Are you two celebrating something? I saw you during the flight. You two look so happy,"

Ferris cuts in, putting his hand on Sloan's back, "Oh just doing a little getaway. You know those Milwaukee winters can be brutal."

"Ah yes," she looks up at both of them. "Well, whatever your reason for coming here, I hope you enjoy yourselves. I sense that you need it. Bye now." She gives a quick wave and walks past them.

"Aww, she was so sweet," Sloan says, looking up at Ferris as they head toward baggage claim. After grabbing their bags and stepping outside, the warm sun greets them like an old friend, wrapping softly around their skin in stark contrast to the biting Milwaukee winter they just left behind. It's an instant reminder of why they needed this. A break. A reset.

Ferris sets his suitcase down beside a bench and sinks onto it, pulling Sloan into his lap with ease. "Now, what do you think we should do while we're here?" he asks, pressing a kiss to her cheek and smiling into her eyes.

"Well, you know I have always wanted to go to Santa Monica Pier," she beams. Just then, their cab pulls up and they stand up to get inside.

"I thought you might say that," he pulls the door open to let Sloan get inside. "Well, let's get checked in at the hotel first and we'll be on our way… tonight."

A few hours later, they arrive at the Santa Monica Pier just as the sun begins to dip below the horizon, casting golden and amber tones across the sky. They step out of the car and head toward the boardwalk. Ferris brushes his forehead, visibly nervous, his eyes darting between Sloan and the bustling scene ahead.

Sloan is immediately enamored by the glow of the sunset reflecting off the ocean, the air warm and salty against her skin. It feels like stepping into a dream. Back home, winter was beginning to creep in—gray skies, snow flurries, and layers of coats—so the change of scenery is like a breath of fresh air.

The pier is alive with laughter and the soft rumble of waves below. Musicians play near the boardwalk's edge while children run past with melting ice cream cones. She gazes out in the distance, watching families and couples soaking up the magic of the evening. The Ferris wheel rotates slowly, its rainbow lights blinking to life as dusk settles, casting playful reflections on the water below.

"Wow, the pier is even more beautiful in person," Sloan's voice is breathy with awe as she takes in the glowing skyline and carnival lights. The soft hues of the sunset catch in her dark hair, and her eyes sparkle as they meet Ferris's.

"I agree. It really couldn't be more perfect," Ferris replies, his voice low, smiling at her—but his gaze lingers just past her shoulder, fixed on the sunset, trying to build up the courage for what comes next.

Sloan turns to look in the direction Ferris is and notices rose petals spread on the pier and lights draped on a small backdrop. "Oh my gosh, it looks like someone's getting proposed to." Her eyes get wide. "Aww, we should move out of the way. Ferris?" She turns to find Ferris on one knee behind her, in disbelief as to what's happening.

Ferris reaches for her hand and holds an open ring box in the other, "Sloan Victoria Bartels, will you marry me?"

Chapter 3

Back in Milwaukee, the sky is the color of wet cement, heavy with the weight of another impending snowstorm. Thick flurries swirl outside the kitchen window as Ted stands at the counter, pouring himself a cup of coffee. He glances toward the living room where Kate sits stiffly on the couch, arms crossed, staring blankly at the muted TV screen. The weather outside mirrored her mood—icy, unpredictable, and slowly piling up.

"Another storm's rolling in," Ted says quietly, more to fill the silence than anything.

Kate doesn't respond. She just blinks at the screen, jaw tight, as if her thoughts are a blizzard of their own. "Ted, they are up to something. I just know it. I just don't trust her." She stands up and starts pacing back and forth in the kitchen.

"One, can you just stop for a minute? You're making me dizzy." Kate turns towards him and brushes her fingers through her hair before Ted continues, "What makes you think they are up to something? And two, what did Sloan ever do, other than make Ferris happy?"

Kate aggressively rolls her eyes. "How do you not see it, Ted? She's changing him. Over the years, he's come to fewer and fewer family functions. And now, Christmas!" She throws her hands in the air. "I suggest making it a family vacation, and they both have a problem with it?" She pauses and puts one hand on her hip and the other scratches her head.

"I mean, to be fair, Sloan didn't say anything... that was Ferris."

"Yeah, but why do you think he's not answering my phone calls now? I bet you she turned his phone off," she shakes her head and looks out the kitchen window. "Ferris never would have done this to me in the past."

***

Sloan feels weak in the knees as she looks down at Ferris, kneeling before her on the soft, sun-warmed sand. The sound of waves crashing gently against the shore fills the air, rhythmic and steady, grounding her in the moment. A warm breeze sweeps past, carrying with it the scent of salt and sunscreen, tousling her hair as if nature itself has paused to witness this moment.

Ferris gently wraps his hand around hers, anchoring her as her heart pounds wildly in her chest. She glances around—blankets and candles carefully placed in the sand, a soft pathway of roses leading back to the boardwalk—but all of it blurred compared to the way he was looking at her.

Suddenly, everything else fades into the background, and it feels as if time has stopped. Was this really happening? Was she dreaming? It seems like she's been standing there staring at him for hours, but she knows it has only been seconds.

"Oh my gosh. How... how did you pull this off?" she whispers, her voice catching as she looks around again, half-expecting someone to jump out from behind a rock or a beach umbrella.

Ferris just smiles up at her, eyes full of love. "I have my ways... so?" He looks down at the ring and back up at her again.

"Yes, of course I'll marry you!" she exclaims, dropping to her knees to kiss him just as he begins to stand. He wraps his arms around her, lifting her into a tight embrace, and for a full minute, they hold each other, lost in the kind of moment you only get once in a lifetime.

"Well, do you want to put it on?" Ferris pulls back for a minute to hand her the ring box and give her a better look.

Sloan's jaw drops and her eyes widen, "Oh my gosh, it's beautiful. Seriously though, how did you pull this all off?"

"I'll let you in on a little secret," Ferris says, lowering his voice playfully. "That guy over there? He doesn't work for the Pier. He sets up secret proposals." He points behind them. "And that woman? That's his wife—she's been taking pictures of us the whole time."

Sloan gasps, eyes wide with surprise. "Mr. Hayes, you sure are something," she says, her voice filled with awe. "And this ring... it's incredible. Did they help you pick it out too?" she laughs, holding up her hand to admire it.

The moment brings back a rush of memories—especially the first time Ferris told her he loved her. It had slipped out accidentally, blurted when he was saying goodbye, but somehow, it was still perfect. They'd been saying 'I love you' ever since.

"Nah," Ferris grins, "I know your style. And I might've called your mom… she may have sent me a few pictures for inspiration."

Sloan shakes her head, grinning. "Well, I don't care what you did. It's perfect—this whole thing is perfect. I'm so excited." She looks down at her ring again, then back at Ferris. "Who should we call first?"

"You know what? I'm going to leave that completely up to you, but if it were up to me, I would say we just enjoy being engaged with no one else knowing until we're at least back home."

"Okay, I love that idea," Sloan leans into Ferris and grabs his face with her hands pulling him in. He wraps his arms around her waist.

***

The next day Jenny pulls up to her parents' house to bring some lunch she picked up. Her heart is pounding, knowing her mom is going to ask her about Ferris again, and at this point, she's run out of things to say. She puts her hand on the doorknob and slowly opens the door before walking inside, right into her parents talking about her brother's whereabouts.

"Honey, have you gotten a hold of Ferris yet?" Ted calls out to his wife.

"No, I've tried three different times now, and it all went right to voicemail. I don't know what's going on," Kate is organizing her hutch in her living room, pulling items out one at a time and holding them up under the light to check for smudges and scratches.

The floorboard creaks under Jenny's foot and Kate turns. "Oh, you're here! Hi, hunny. Now what do I owe you for lunch?"

Jenny gives a quick wave and smile before walking through the living room and getting everything set up on the kitchen counter. "Nothing, Mom, it's my treat." She grabs a to-go box out of the bag and slides it across the counter to indicate it's for her mom. She then grabs her own box and brings it over to the kitchen table to start eating.

"Hey, Jenny, so I wanna give you one last chance to let me know, are you coming on vacation or not?" Kate has her laptop pulled up next to her at the kitchen table with flights and hotels on the screen.

"No, Mom, I'm not coming on the vacation that Ferris did not invite us to," Jenny picks up her burger and takes a big bite, immediately following it with a sip of Sprite.

"All right, well, you snooze, you lose. I'm gonna go ahead and book it right now," Kate turns towards the computer screen and scrolls a few seconds before she clicks, "Done!" She turns to Jenny, waiting for her approval.

"Don't say I didn't warn you."

"It's Christmas, Jenny, the family should be together!"

"Well, one day, Ferris is gonna start his own family, and what are you gonna do then?" Jenny grabs a fry and dips it in ketchup.

"What do you mean, what am I gonna do then?" Kate gazes at Jenny, her eyebrows raised in disbelief, wondering how a thought like that could even cross her mind. "He's still going to be in my family. He will obviously bring the kids here for the holidays."

"Right, but his wife, who hopefully will be Sloan, and any kids they might have, will come before you."

"Oh, don't be silly. You can never replace your mother," Kate puts her hand dramatically on her heart with a self-satisfied smirk as if she were the epitome of perfection.

Annoyance runs across Jenny's face as she presses her hands on her cheeks and murmurs, "I don't think he's looking to replace his mother."

Kate takes another bite of her sandwich and throws the rest back down on the plate before shoving the to-go box away and standing up, "Ugh, Jenny, you just don't understand. One day when you have kids of your own, you'll know what I mean. Now, I have to go, I have my yoga class in fifteen minutes."

Kate grabs her water bottle from the table and walks to the stairs so she can do her yoga from the basement. Jenny continues picking at her fries for the next couple of minutes, picking them up one by one, investigating their appearance, and taking an exhausted bite. When she decides she's had enough, she grabs the garbage from the table and tosses it out. She's losing more and more of her patience as each day passes.

Chapter 4

Even the most busy and chaotic cities can look peaceful from an airplane. Ferris smiles as he looks out the window and sees the cars parading around the city skyscrapers. It helps him feel more at ease about coming back home and breaking the news to his parents, well, more so his mother. She's always had a habit of playing the victim and he knows that the second he tells her she'll make it about herself. This was how the proposal needed to go, though, and each day it became more and more clear that his mom would just show up at the drop of a hat, he'd needed to make sure it was special for just the two of them.

"Well, here we are, back in Milwaukee, ready to face the real world," Ferris looks away from the window, shifts his focus to Sloan's face, and reaches over to squeeze her thigh.

Sloan gives a small smirk and lets out a sigh, "While I do want to live in Dreamland a little bit longer, I'm so excited to finally tell family and friends we're engaged." The captain turns off the seatbelt sign, so Sloan stands up to get her suitcase from the overhead compartment.

As they get to the car, Ferris turns his phone off of airplane mode and sees texts and voice messages coming in from his mom. He lets out a huge sigh before picking up his phone to call her back.

"Hey, Mom. Sorry, I missed your call. What's going on?"

"Oh my God, Ferris, you're alive!" Kate blurts, loud enough to alert the entire neighborhood. "Was your phone broken or something?"

"No, Sloan and I just decided to do a weekend without phones," he lies.

"Hmm. I'm not sure I buy that. But you'd tell me if someone was *making* you turn your phone off, right?"

"What? No, Mom. Sloan is not making me turn my phone off, okay?"

From the passenger seat, Sloan glances over and rolls her eyes, clearly unimpressed.

"I was just checking because I care."

"Sure, Mom." Ferris presses his lips together. "Anyway, I was hoping Sloan and I could swing by next week."

"Oh really? And why's that?"

"I was wondering if we could borrow that extra luggage set you have for our trip," Ferris says, glancing at Sloan and wishing he'd come up with a more solid excuse.

"Don't you have your own luggage?"

"Yeah, but the zipper broke on mine during my last work trip. I haven't had a chance to replace it," he answers quickly, though they both know that never happened.

A pause.

"Well, if you're just picking up luggage, why don't you come alone? I'll cook your favorite meal. Besides, I'm sure Sloan would enjoy some time to herself."

She delivers it sweetly like she's doing Sloan a favor, but Ferris knows her real motive—she wants to get him alone. She wants to talk him out of proposing.

He ignores the suggestion, simply repeating, "So, about the luggage..."

"Fine," Kate replies, reluctantly. "I guess you can borrow it."

She debates mentioning the trip she just secretly booked—but decides it'll be more fun to drop that bomb in person.

***

The following week, Sloan and Ferris pulled up in his parents' driveway, their hearts pounding with a mix of excitement and nerves. While his parents already had the Christmas tree up at Thanksgiving, the house was now fully decked out in Christmas lights and decorations on the outside, complete with a Santa, a sleigh, and eight tiny reindeer in the yard.

Ferris and Sloan were seconds from getting out of the car so they could get in and share the news of their engagement—but the anticipation of his parent's reactions made them both uneasy.

"So, your mom has no clue?" Sloan asks, her voice tight as she steps out of the car.

"Nope," Ferris replies, shutting his car door behind him. "I told my parents I was going to propose at some point, but I never mentioned when. They had no idea I already had the ring—or a plan." He tries to sound confident, but deep down, he isn't sure if his mom would be more upset about the proposal or the Santa Monica trip. Either way, it had to be this way. After how she reacted—and tried to invite herself along—he'd had to move quickly.

Sloan glances down at her ring, watching it catch the light as a wave of uneasiness settles over her. Ferris's mom has always been a little unpredictable. If things are going her way, she's all fake smiles and compliments—but the second she's lost control? All bets are off.

Ferris steps up behind Sloan and gently squeezes her shoulders. "It's going to be okay," he says quietly. "I promise. Oh wait, I forgot something." With that, Ferris quickly runs back to the car and grabs a bouquet of flowers he had sitting in the backseat, something to sweeten the blow to his mom. He rejoins Sloan, and the two of them walk up to the house together.

"We're here!" He calls out as he opens the door.

"Ferris! My handsome boy—it's so good to see you!" Kate rushes to the door, breezing right past Sloan as she wraps her arms tightly around her son. "Oh my! Are these gorgeous flowers for me?" she coos, already grabbing the bouquet from Ferris's hands before he can answer. "Hi, Sloan." Without waiting for a response, Kate gives her a quick, tight-lipped smile and a light tap on the shoulder before gliding back toward the kitchen.

"Wine, anyone?" Kate calls over her shoulder as if the entrance hadn't just been hijacked.

"Mom, you seem to be upbeat tonight. What's going on?"

"Well, I'm just really looking forward to things," she answers as she grabs the wine opener and starts fidgeting with the bottle.

"Like what?"

"Well, Christmas is right around the corner. We're doing something a little different this year. It's kind of fun, right Sloan?" Kate says as she hands Sloan a glass of wine.

Sloan hesitantly reaches out to grab it, thinking to herself she should have paid more attention to Kate pouring to make sure she didn't poison it.

"Oh yeah? What's your plan, Mom?" Ferris knew the inevitable was coming.

"Well," she stops and looks directly at Sloan again, "Sloan, I know you're trying to keep my son away from me this Christmas, but you can't get rid of me because I just booked a trip to Santa Monica too!" She throws her hands in the air, looking around and waiting for the others to join in her excitement.

Ted just stands there behind her, silently, knowing this is all wrong.

Ferris feels his jaw tighten and looks over at Sloan. She audibly sighs and rolls her eyes as the familiar frustration washes over her. Of course, she had expected this. The news wasn't surprising—just tiresome, like hearing the same broken record on repeat. "What?" is all Ferris can say.

Kate starts nodding profusely, sipping her wine, "Yep! Dad's coming too. It was gonna be a surprise, but I saw your faces and I just knew I couldn't hold it in anymore!"

"Mom, um, I don't know how to say this, but..."

Kate cuts him off, "Look, I know what you're going to say, but I was thinking about it, and Sloan, cover your ears, but you're going to need an extra person there when everything's going down." Sloan looks over at Ferris and back at his mom. "I have a good camera."

Ferris firmly tells his mom, "Stop! You're not coming to Santa Monica with us, and I need you to respect that."

Kate blinks. Once. Twice. Her mouth opens, then closes. She lowers her wine glass like it's suddenly too heavy to hold and slams it on the table.

Part 2

Chapter 5

Splashes from the wine slowly make their way to the kitchen table as Kate stands at a crossroads between Ferris and Sloan. "What do you mean we're not going to Santa Monica?"

"Did you actually not hear me, or are you still confused?" Ferris asks, his voice edged with frustration. He could hardly believe the words coming out of his own mouth. He's never stood up to his mom quite like this and now he's questioning whether or not he's coming on too strong. It feels like years of resentment over how she's controlled him are all coming out at once.

Kate looks at him, searching for a response, but no words come. She blinks a few times before Ferris rearranges his words, slower this time, "We aren't going to Santa Monica for Christmas anymore."

Kate squints and tilts her head, trying to process his words. Her face tilts, her expression changing rapidly from confused to personally attacked. "How could you do this to me?" she accuses, her voice rising. "First, you try to tell me you won't be around for Christmas," she makes sure to glare at Sloan when she says this, "Then, I jump on board and get excited after you tried to abandon me. I plan everything, I buy tickets, and now–"

"Well, Mom, why would you just buy tickets for *my* vacation when I told you that you weren't invited in the first place?" Ferris's pacing becomes more agitated, each step quicker than the last. His tone sharpens with each word, and Sloan stands awkwardly nearby, watching as his fists clench and unclench at his sides.

Sloan's stomach twists. The room feels smaller with Kate in it, like her mere presence is sucking the air out of every corner.

"Well, I just didn't understand why you wouldn't want Dad and me to be a part of your Christmas," Kate stands in the kitchen as she starts to open up her laptop, clicking away in a panic.

"Because it was a trip for the two of us," Ferris stops to take a breath and look over at Sloan, who's visibly doing everything she can to not jump in.

"Okay, but now you aren't going? My tickets are non-refundable, so what are we supposed to do?" Kate plops herself down on the couch and pouts like a toddler not getting their way.

Ted walks over and gently chimes in, his voice cracking with desperation. "Kate, look, I told you not to do this."

"Oh, come on—you said it would be fun too," she snaps, not even turning to look at him. Ted raises his eyebrows, clearly at a loss for words.

"Mom, I'm sorry—but it's not my fault you bought non-refundable tickets after I *clearly* told you not to come." Ferris's mouth feels dry, the words sharp on his tongue. His hands tighten at his sides, bracing for the fallout.

In the chaos of the conversation, Ferris has completely forgotten that there's even bigger news to share. A chill runs down his spine. He instantly grows fearful of what's coming next.

Over the years, he'd started telling her less and less. Every time he tried to hold onto something joyful, she would find a way to snatch it away. Excitement, pride, progress—if it didn't involve her, she found a way to ruin it. She'd meet him with fear, disappointment, or loaded questions about his life choices. Always.

Then it happens. A sudden spark of realization crosses Kate's face, and her expression shifts to something sharper—curiosity wrapped in suspicion. "So, wait... why aren't you going now?" she asks slowly.

She pauses, then turns her head with a smirk, her voice dripping with condescension.

"Sloan, did my words finally get to you? Did you realize the hurt you've caused my family?"

As Kate leans in slightly, Sloan catches a faint whiff of wine on her breath—rich and sour, like trouble about to spill.

Sloan glances at Ferris, silently pleading for backup. But he's frozen, eyes wide, still trying to process the chaos unraveling in front of him. She turns back to Kate and clears her throat. "Uh, no. Like I said—the trip wasn't my idea." But even as she says it, a familiar feeling creeps in. Sloan thinks of everything Kate has said over the years—the condescending remarks, the backhanded compliments. And now? Kate's not even pretending anymore. She doesn't think Sloan is good enough for Ferris, and she's not afraid to say it out loud.

Kate crosses her arms, her eyes narrowing. "Right. Sure. Okay, so… Ferris, what's going on? Why aren't you going?" She shoots him a suspicious look, then shifts her gaze back to Sloan, like the answer must be hidden somewhere within her.

"Well…," Ferris starts to answer before he takes a deep breath, looking down at the floor.

A look of relief washes over her face. "Oh my gosh, wait!" She's wide-eyed and starts to stand up and walk closer to Ferris, "Oh, my boy! You couldn't go through with it." She clenched her fist and jerked it close to her body like a small celebration she was trying to keep to herself.

Sloan furrows her brows, turning from Kate to Ferris. "What is she talking about?" Her face burns, heat rising from her chest to her cheeks. Without thinking, she slides the hair tie off her wrist and pulls her hair into a ponytail—*the same way someone would before a fight*. Not for vanity, but for clarity. Control. Readiness.

Kate slowly starts to turn back toward Sloan. She raises an eyebrow as her lips curve into a smug smirk, as if humoring a child, "Oh, honey, see, my son was about to make a huge mistake, and his father and I stopped him." She smiles proudly, pats the table next to Sloan, and walks over towards Ted. His arms are crossed tightly, gaze drifting toward the door, avoiding eye contact as a heavy sigh escapes his lips.

Sloan shows almost no emotion. She's dealt with Kate hating her and putting her down for the last couple of years. This isn't new, although she's not sure if her treatment will be different once Kate knows the truth. It feels like being out in the wild—when a predator steps into view, you either freeze, play dead, or fight for your life. She was still deciding which path would keep her safest.

Ted quickly shuts Kate down. "Oh, no, do not bring me into this." He immediately turns away from her and walks in the other direction, out of the living room and towards his office.

Ferris isn't dumb, he knows exactly where his mom is going with this. "Okay, I'm going to stop you right there. The reason we're not going to Santa Monica is because that's where we went last weekend." He turns to look at Sloan. She smiles back with nervousness in her eyes.

Kate furrows her brow, as though concentrating harder will make his words clearer. "I'm sorry, you did *what* last weekend?" She leans forward, trying to make sense of what she thinks she just heard.

Ferris walks over to Sloan, wrapping his arm around her shoulders. "We took a spontaneous trip to Santa Monica." He gives her shoulders a good squeeze, silently letting her know he's got her back.

"And you couldn't have called me and told me you were doing this?" Kate throws her arms up in the air, her eyes suspiciously bouncing between Ferris and Sloan.

"What'd I miss? I hear a lot of yelling over here," Jenny, Ferris's sister, hurtles into the kitchen as if her favorite show was about to start. Her long hair bounces as she plops onto the counter to get a front-row seat.

Kate whips around, sulking, "Oh, just your brother telling us that he went to Santa Monica spontaneously last weekend. Did you know?"

Jenny looks at her mom, wide-eyed. She wasn't sure if she was supposed to admit to knowing they went or play dumb. She was going to go with playing dumb. "Wow! You guys went to Santa Monica last weekend? That's amazing. I thought you looked like you guys had a little sunkissed glow there."

Kate, doing what she always does, grasps at anyone to get them on her side. "Jenny, now is not the time for small talk. Ferris, I just don't understand why you went last week when you told us all you were going for Christmas. Do you like playing games with us?"

Jenny hops off the counter and walks over to the pantry to grab a bag of chips, returning promptly to the counter without missing a beat.

"Yeah, actually, I had the trip planned for last weekend the whole time. But I knew the second I told you we were going to Santa Monica, you'd find some way to come along," he says, his tone steady at first. But as the words leave his mouth, a flicker of guilt creeps in. His voice trembles near the end—not because he regrets the decision, but because he hates that it had to come to this.

Kate's face is beyond shocked, "I don't believe this." She looks over at Jenny again waiting for a sign that she's not crazy.

Jenny looks back at her mom, finishes chewing, and says, "Well, I mean... he's got a point for doing this to you." She pauses. "I mean, I can't really blame him." She gives Ferris a quick wink.

It's at that moment Ted starts to wander back into the kitchen, casually standing on the other side of the counter next to Jenny—involuntarily picking sides.

"Jenny, that's enough from you," Kate snaps, her tone sharp.

Jenny gives her a look that clearly says, *Then why'd you ask me?* But she stays silent, letting it go.

Ted decides to walk forward now and change up the mood, "All right, so we established that they went to Santa Monica. I think that's pretty cool." He turns and looks right at Kate before turning back to his son and Sloan. "So, how was your trip, guys?"

"Ted, could you not right now?" Kate looks as if she's disappointed by her entire family. "So, if you went to Santa Monica last weekend, why did you call me about borrowing my luggage?"

Ferris flashes a grin, his eyes sparkling with excitement as he leans in closer to Sloan, his hand resting lightly on her back. "Well, because we actually have some really exciting news to share with you guys." He glances at her, a playful glint in his eye. "Sloan, you want to do the honors?"

Sloan looks at Ferris, questioning everything—*Is now really the right time?* Her hands are clammy, her heart pounding. What she always imagined would be a joyful, celebrated milestone now feels uncertain and exposed.

Ferris senses her hesitation and gently takes her hand. The warmth of his touch calms her nerves almost instantly. He gives her a reassuring smile, then nods toward her ring.

Sloan takes a deep breath and flashes a big smile. She rotates her hand and holds it up to show off the beautiful addition on her finger. "We got engaged!" she announces, her voice excited—though still a little shaky.

Kate's expression freezes. Her eyes go wide, locked in disbelief.

The room grows quiet. Jenny stares at her mom, giving her the opportunity to reply kindly, although she looks like she's going to combust.

Ted is the first to break the silence and walks over to hug Ferris and Sloan, "Oh congratulations, son! Sloan, this is amazing. Welcome to the family."

"No way!" Jenny exclaims, taking it all in before tossing down the bag of chips. She strides over to Sloan, grabs her hand to admire the ring, and pulls her into a big hug. "Oh, I'm so excited! I had a feeling—I just knew it. I can't wait to have a sister!"

Sloan beams with joy, and the two giggle together, marveling at the ring.

Kate just stands there, motionless, as a look of disgust slowly pours over her face. She opens her mouth once... then again... but nothing comes out. Her breath feels short. Her face, hot.

Finally, she manages to force out a few words. "Sister? This is a joke, right?"

There's no way she's hearing this correctly. She must've had too much wine. She needs her blood pressure meds—and maybe a call to her chiropractor.

"No, we actually got engaged," Ferris quickly assured her.

Kate's eyes go wide while she looks around the room like someone drowning looking for a floating device.

"Mom, are you good?" His mom had always had a lot to say, and right now she seems to be holding it all in... but the explosion would happen any minute.

"I'm just a little confused," Kate says, her voice rising with emotion. "You're telling me you had this big moment—this milestone in your life—and you excluded your own mother from it?"

She was finally starting to spill—and going to have a hard time cleaning up the mess.

Sloan's excitement fades in an instant. She gently pulls her hand from Jenny's and hides it behind her back, suddenly embarrassed for ever letting herself feel excited. It reminds her of the time Ferris brought a cake to his parents' house to celebrate her birthday. Kate had quickly shut it down, reminding him *her* birthday was *last week*—and that it was silly to celebrate again.

"I'm sorry," Ferris says, visibly trying to hold his composure, "where exactly do you think *you* fit into the equation of *me* proposing to my girlfriend?"

Kate starts to walk towards him with panic in her eyes, "I could have been there filming. I could have been there helping set up something!" At this point, everyone in the room is just staring at her, dumbfounded. "I would have just liked to be in the know about it. Sorry for wanting to be involved and make it a beautiful day for you." Kate looks down like a dog that just had an accident in the house, the only difference being this was no accident. She knew exactly what she was doing.

Ferris takes a deep breath before saying, "Look, Mom, I don't know if you remember this or not, but I actually did tell you I was gonna propose, and what was your reaction?" He lifts his eyebrows and throws his hands out as if to say *you can't win here*.

Kate pauses and looks around like she's trying to find the right answer somewhere in the room, "Well, I was initially shocked, as any mother would be, you can't blame me for that." Her voice softens at the end of her sentence as she draws a small smile to try and remind him that they're on the same team.

Ferris's jaw tightens as a vein pulses in his temple, his breath coming in shallow bursts. His fists clench so tightly that his knuckles turn white, his face flushed crimson, like he's holding back a tidal wave of words. Finally, the wave crashes. "No! No, you weren't shocked. You were rude. You completely dismissed my ability to make a decision as an adult. You were rude to Sloan. You put down our relationship, and then you invited yourself to be a part of our trip after doing all of that. How can you not see how asinine this all is?" Ferris walks away to the living room couch to sit down.

Sloan puts her hand on her head as if to unfurrow her eyebrow while keeping her eyes closed and takes a deep breath. She then walks over to sit beside Ferris, putting her hand on his leg.

Kate is not even phased by his anger. She's the real victim here, so why would she back down. "Well, what does it even matter? You lied the whole time anyway, so it wasn't even a real trip." She purses her lips as she picks up her phone and starts scrolling through.

"Well, lucky for us, I did lie and plan accordingly because I know you. Otherwise, you would have ruined the whole surprise," Ferris speaks much calmer this time around. "I mean, you literally brought up the engagement when we walked in before you knew any of this happened." Ferris puts his hand to his head and starts rubbing his forehead profusely.

Kate, still looking at her phone, mumbles, "I did not. There's no way she would have known that's what I was talking about." She pauses to look up at the ceiling before lowering her tone and speaking again. "I should have known this was going to happen." Kate stands up and walks over to the couch, looking directly at Sloan this time, "Don't you see what you're doing to my family? You must be so proud taking a son away from his mother."

"Look, I'm sorry, but I've heard enough from you." Sloan stands up, the words spilling out before she can stop them. Her voice is steady, but her hands tremble. "For the last time, I have *not* taken your son away from you. He's a grown man—he can make his own decisions."

Ferris rises to stand beside her. Sloan reaches for his hand and grips it tightly, her knuckles turning white.

Kate lets out a long exhale and walks over to the fridge to fill up her water bottle, nonchalantly saying, "Well, he never would have done this in the past. So, you tell me what or who the issue here is."

Sloan mouths, "I'm done," to Ferris and walks over to the front door. As she slips on her coat, she turns back to Kate. "Yeah, well... maybe you should start looking in the mirror," Sloan says coolly. "You might just find your answer there."

Ferris follows her, stepping in front of her like a shield. "Mom, you need to stop pointing the finger at everyone else—especially at Sloan—and start taking some responsibility."

Kate looks down as if his words have physically struck her.

Sloan reaches around Ferris, gesturing toward Kate to make her point even clearer. "*You're* the one causing all the issues here. *You're* the one pushing your son away."

Kate looks at Ted, hoping—*expecting*—him to step in, to defend her. But he just stands there, arms crossed, leaning against the doorway with a tired look in his eyes. He's said his piece. He's not getting in the middle of this one.

"I will not be talked to that way in my own house," she snaps, her voice shaking more than she'd like.

Ferris places his hand on Sloan's back, gently guiding her toward the door. "Well, that's no problem, Mom, because we're leaving now."

He thanks his dad and Jenny for their congratulations and quickly apologizes for the abrupt exit before stepping outside.

Jenny—wishing she had just stayed home—rushes over to give them both a hug. She whispers a quiet, "I'm sorry," even though she knows she has nothing to apologize for. It's not guilt—it's the helplessness of not being able to stop any of this.

Kate starts to sniffle and moves in for a hug from Ferris, but he turns away, placing a hand on his dad's back instead—a clear, silent boundary.

Sloan heads out the door first, Ferris following close behind. But just before they reach the steps, Sloan spins around and walks right back up to the doorway—making sure she's technically still outside. "We'll be seeing you... maybe." She pauses for a beat, "Now that I'm on the porch and not in your house—keep this up, and you just might not get an invite to the wedding after all."

Chapter 6

After weeks of planning, Jenny had finally pulled together all the details for Ferris and Sloan's engagement party. Despite their repeated insistence that it wasn't necessary, she had refused to take no for an answer. Truthfully, she needed something big to look forward to. Between the demands of school and work, life had been overwhelming. Seeing a new guy had given her a glimmer of hope, but what she really needed was a distraction—and this party was the perfect one.

On the morning of the party, Jenny woke up early to bake cupcakes for the dessert table. The warm, sweet smell filled her home. She'd even managed to make custom ring toppers that read *F&S*.

Was it because she genuinely cared? Or was she overcompensating for the fact that her mom wasn't invited? She wasn't sure. But either way, she was excited to do this for them.

Sloan had quickly become like a sister to Jenny. Growing up with just one brother had its perks—she always had someone to back her up, someone to joke around with—but Jenny had always longed for that special bond she saw in movies, the one between sisters. She wanted someone who could understand her on a deeper level, someone who would share in the highs and lows of life with her.

She still remembers the day Ferris brought Sloan home to meet their parents. It wasn't the first time Ferris had introduced a girlfriend to the family—he'd had a steady stream of women in his life, all of whom seemed to come and go without leaving much of a mark. Ferris was charming, good-looking, athletic, and easy to get along with, so it made sense that he always had someone around. But somehow, none of the relationships ever seemed to stick... until Sloan.

Sloan was different. She had an air of uniqueness that made her stand out—yet, she was also kind, easy to talk to, and effortlessly interesting. From the moment Jenny met her, she could tell that Sloan wasn't just another girl Ferris was dating. There was something about her that made everyone want to be around her. She had a quiet strength, a warmth that made you feel seen, and a way of making everyone feel like they were important.

Sloan became more than just Ferris's girlfriend—she became someone Jenny could rely on. With how their mom had been treating Sloan lately she knew she needed to do everything in her power to protect Sloan and let her know she was on her side.

***

By the time afternoon rolls around, over at Sloan and Ferris's house, the air feels thick with anticipation. Sloan stands in front of the bathroom mirror, her palms pressed against the cold countertop. The faint scent of lavender soap clings to the air, mingling with the sharper edge of Ferris's minty toothpaste.

She takes a slow, shaky breath, watching her chest rise in the mirror, trying to appear calm, even if her stomach twists in knots. Her fingers tremble as she smooths a strand of hair behind her ear. The faint hum of the bathroom fan is the only sound breaking the silence between them.

Ferris finishes brushing his teeth and leans over the sink to spit. The water runs briefly, and he glances sideways at her, eyes narrowing with concern. He wipes his mouth with a towel and sets it down gently like he doesn't want to disturb whatever's going on in her head.

"I cannot believe that after everything, your mom thinks she should still be invited to the engagement party," Sloan says, her voice strained. She dabs blush on her cheeks and runs her fingers through her hair, trying to distract herself.

It was true. The past few weeks had been a whirlwind of calls and texts from Kate, all about the engagement party, including one last night as a last-ditch effort to be a part of the set-up. After the big blowout that night, Kate had acted as though nothing had happened. The very next morning, she called Ferris to talk about wedding plans, completely ignoring the tension. Not once did she ask how Sloan was doing or call to apologize. Ferris, unwilling to deal with her antics, found excuses to avoid her calls or cut them short after that.

To Sloan's surprise, Kate and Ted canceled their planned trip to Santa Monica for Christmas. Kate claimed she wanted the family together, but Ferris and Sloan, still reeling from the turmoil, opted to spend the holidays with Sloan's mom and extended family instead.

When Kate heard Jenny was hosting an engagement party, she immediately tried to take control. She started a Pinterest board and began mentally planning how to decorate her house for the event, assuming it would be hosted there.

"What do you mean I can't come? It'll be at my house!" Kate protested, her voice rising as she gripped the edge of the kitchen counter. The sharp scent of citrus cleaning spray hung in the air, a reminder of her constant need for control. Her nails clicked against the marble, trying to keep pace with her racing thoughts.

"No, Mom," Jenny replied firmly, crossing her arms and standing her ground. *"After everything that's happened, Ferris and Sloan made it clear they don't want you at the engagement party."*

Kate's eyes widened, and she took a deep, quick breath as if inhaling the bitter taste of defeat. *"But... this isn't fair!"* she protested, her words trembling with the weight of her disbelief.

Jenny's expression remained unmoved. Her tone was measured as she continued, *"Mom, there's nothing you can say to change my mind. The more you push, the more you'll find yourself left out of things. If I were you, I'd accept it... and move on."*

At that moment, the kitchen was filled with an undercurrent of unspoken resentment—an emotional friction that had been simmering for weeks, now made palpable in every measured word and silent pause.

In the bathroom, Ferris sighs and looks at Sloan in the mirror. "I know, nothing gets through to her. Honestly, an engagement party feels completely unnecessary, but after everything, you deserve it."

Sloan shrugs, her expression softening. "We deserve it, plus it will be special being able to celebrate with our family and friends." She puts a strong emphasis on "we" and turns her body around to give Ferris a long, warm embrace.

He puts both hands on her face, leaning in for a soft kiss that quickly deepens, but before they can lose themselves in it, there's a knock at the front door and a "Guys! I'm here!"

Ferris pops his head out into the hall and sees that Jenny let herself in with a tray of cupcakes and a couple bags hanging on her arms.

"I'm just going to go ahead and set up. Don't peek! Just relax and enjoy yourselves—it'll all be ready in about half an hour," Jenny flashes a nervous smile.

"Thanks again for doing this," Ferris says warmly. "You sure you don't need any help?"

"Nope! You know I love doing this kind of thing. Plus, the new guy I'm seeing, Charlie, is coming by in a little bit, so I won't be alone."

"Charlie? Kiss in the rain guy? Oooh, I can't wait to meet him," Sloan pops her head out quickly to see the look on Jenny's face.

"Kiss in the rain guy?" Ferris is confused.

"It's a long story. Girl talk. You won't get it," Sloan laughs as she goes back to her room to finish her makeup.

Ferris rolls his eyes and steps outside toward Jenny's car to help carry in the rest of the decorations. The early afternoon sun is high and bright, casting long shadows across the driveway. A warm breeze drifts through the quiet neighborhood—unusual for this time of year, but welcome.

When he returns inside, arms full, he sets the bags down and uses the moment to casually ask, "Did, uh... Mom say anything else to you?"

Jenny, continuing to carry in a box, looks exhausted. Holding the boundaries in your family is a full-time job. "Yeah, I mean, honestly, she's asked about it every single day. I keep telling her it's not up to me, but I have a feeling she's gonna come with Dad."

Those words hit Ferris like a knife to the chest. "Seriously? After telling her no over one hundred times. So, what do we do if that happens?"

Jenny sets the box down on the kitchen counter and then turns to Ferris. Her voice is calm, steady. "Just carry on like it's nothing. Don't give it energy. Acknowledge her, then move on—and whatever you do, protect Sloan. Always."

"That's good advice, but if she says anything, I do not have a problem kicking her out."

"Ay ay, captain," Jenny gives a crisp salute, "Well, for now, I'm going to have to kick you out because I have to set up!"

Ferris and Sloan head to their room to hide out while Jenny sets up.

***

Finally, about thirty minutes later, Jenny knocks at their bedroom door with a smile in her voice, "Ferris, Sloan, you're free to come out."

Ferris is the first to step through the door, leading them down the hallway. The warm, savory scent of baked brie and garlic crostini hits them immediately, mingling with something sweet—maybe cinnamon from the mini apple tarts cooling on the dessert table.

Jenny completely outdid herself. There are balloons, a custom *Ferris & Sloan* sign, and a fully decked-out dessert spread that looks like it belongs in a magazine photoshoot.

"Oh my gosh, Jenny, this looks amazing," Sloan says, eyes wide as she takes it all in.

"How did you do this so quickly?"

"Well, the half an hour here, and I won't even get into how much time I spent prepping all this. Plus, I had some help."

She winks, stepping aside so Ferris can see his best friend, Callum, behind her.

Callum pulls Ferris in for a firm, no-frills hug—one of those shoulder-clasping, back-patting embraces that says everything without needing a word. When they pull apart, Callum gives a crooked grin and quickly shoves his hands into his pockets, like he doesn't quite know what to do with them. He has a bit of uneven stubble along his jaw, the kind that looked less intentional and more like he'd forgotten to shave for a couple of days.

Callum was more than a best friend; he was the closest thing Ferris ever had to a brother.

Their bond had started back in middle school when Callum took a seat next to Ferris on the bus. The other kids had teased Callum about his glasses, and the very next day, Ferris showed up wearing an identical pair. Ferris had a cool way about him that made the other kids envious. So, once they saw him do that, the bullying stopped. From that moment on, Ferris had always felt a quiet, unwavering protectiveness over his friend.

"Thanks for coming, Callum. It's so good to see you."

"Yeah, it's been too long, I've been so busy," Callum turns to look at Sloan. "And you're looking beautiful as ever."

He pulls her into a big bear hug, and as Sloan leans in, she catches sight of a woman standing behind him. With short strawberry-blonde hair and a sharp glare directed her way, the woman's expression is anything but welcoming. Beside her, a little girl—no older than three or four—tugs impatiently at her shirt, her small fingers curling into the fabric.

The woman clears her throat loud enough for everyone to hear. Sloan pulls away from Callum, feeling she may have overstepped.

Callum quickly turns towards the woman as his cheeks turn rosy, "Oh, sorry, honey." He turns back to Ferris and Sloan, "This is my new girlfriend, Gretchen. I really wanted you guys to meet her."

Gretchen gives a small, uncertain smile, "Nice to meet you." She still looks slightly annoyed, like she has somewhere better to be.

Ferris, feeling the awkwardness in the room, tries to make conversation. "Thanks for coming, Gretchen. I've heard a lot about you."

The truth was, he hadn't heard much at all. Callum had a habit of getting completely wrapped up in whoever he was dating—like they became his entire personality. When he'd talked about Gretchen, it was vague at best. Everything he said sounded like it could've been about any girl before her.

Sloan is making goofy faces at the little girl, trying to make her laugh, "And who is this little one?"

Gretchen looks down like she forgot she had someone else with her, "Oh, this is my daughter, Christy."

"Well, hi, Christy. Nice to meet you," Ferris crouches down to her level.

Christy looks up and hides behind Gretchen's leg before walking over to Callum and pulling on his arm.

Ferris continues, "Well, guys, there's food and drinks over here that my sister set up, so not really sure what's there, but help yourselves."

Guests start arriving in steady waves, their laughter and conversation gradually filling the house with a light buzz. The savory smell of baked brie and garlic crostini still hangs in the air, though the trays are already looking sparse—people clearly broke into them the moment they walked in. A few guests hover near the kitchen island with plates in hand, chatting between bites, while others gather near the drink station. The mini apple tarts are nearly gone too, a clear hit. The space was warm, lively, and finally starting to feel like a celebration.

As the greetings settle and conversations pick up around them, Ferris turns to Callum. "Hey, do you have a quick sec?" he asked, nodding toward the hallway.

"Yeah, sure. What's going on?" He puts Christy down and gestures for Gretchen to take her to grab a drink. Meanwhile, Sloan walks over to Jenny to greet and talk to some other guests.

"Okay, so you probably knew this was coming, but I wanted to just do this before it got crazy." Ferris turns to grab a box off the kitchen table and hands it to Callum. "This is for you."

Callum takes the box and starts to open it carefully. "Oh man, let me see." He pulls out a bottle of whiskey, and as it leaves the box, a small card falls out. Callum picks it up off the floor and reads the inside out loud, "Callum, will you be my best man?"

"Nah, I'm busy," Callum laughs. "Of course, I'll be your best man." He gives Ferris a pat on the back.

"I know, I know, it's a little cheesy. But the card was Sloan's idea." Ferris smirks, "It's a little early because we don't have the wedding date set yet, but we're gonna have a really small wedding party, so we just wanna let everyone know now."

The two friends chat together for a few more minutes before they hear a crash and realize Gretchen's daughter Christy had been climbing over near the drinks. Callum looks embarrassed before rushing over to take care of her.

Ferris turns around to see his dad walking through the front door, his mom quietly trying to sneak in behind his dad. Anger takes over Ferris's whole body.

"What is she doing here?" Sloan's voice comes from just behind Ferris as she steps beside him, stopping in her tracks. The look on her face says it all—like every ounce of excitement had been drained, leaving her expression blank and unreadable.

Chapter 7

"I—I don't know," Ferris stammers. "I swear, she wasn't invited. Jenny said she had a feeling she might show up with my dad."

Why hadn't he locked the door—or at least warned Sloan? He'd be asking himself that for the rest of the night.

Sloan rolls her eyes, clearly irritated that Kate has no respect for her boundaries. "Well, she has to leave. I'm not going to be dealing with this tension at my own engagement party."

"Yes, I know. Jenny suggested we should pretend like she's not even here, carry on, and have fun. That will make her more mad than anything. We just can't feed into it."

Sloan scoffs. "Fine, but she better not say anything to me." With a slow inhale, she drops her chin to her chest before rolling her head to one side, then the other, as if shaking off the anxiety. "Speaking of Jenny, do you know where she is? I want to give the gift to her before your mom takes away my joy," she pauses, "I mean, before I get too distracted."

"Did I hear my name?" Just then, Jenny appears like she'd been summoned.

"Yeah, so before this turns into a real party and I get too distracted, I have something for you," Sloan picks up a small gold bag from their kitchen table.

"I said no gifts! I did this party as a treat for you." Jenny pushes the bag away.

"Just open it," Sloan rolls her eyes and pushes it back.

Jenny carefully pulls out the tissue paper before revealing a small jewelry box and card, reading it. "Wait, what? Will you be my maid of honor? Sloan, of course!" She wraps her arms around Sloan.

"Wait you didn't even open the gift yet, what if it was coal?" Sloan laughs.

"I don't care, still saying yes," Jenny says as she opens the jewelry box, revealing a beautiful gold necklace. "It's absolutely gor—"

"I didn't realize there was a gift exchange going on."

Sloan turns to see Kate standing right behind her, a bottle of champagne in hand. Sloan awkwardly smiles and turns back to Jenny, hoping she'll take it from there because she doesn't want to waste her breath.

"It's not a gift exchange, Mom. Sloan just asked me to be her maid of honor."

Kate raises her eyebrows and looks at Sloan like has mud all over her face. "Don't you usually ask a friend of yours to be a maid of honor?"

Jenny cuts in, "We are friends, Mom, and we'll be sisters pretty soon." She smiles and puts her arm around Sloan.

"Sisters-in-*law*," Kate emphasizes. "Anyways, I brought this champagne for you." She extends the bottle toward Sloan, arm outstretched, waiting for her to take it.

"My mom just got here," Sloan says abruptly, turning to walk away without so much as a glance at Kate—or the bottle.

Kate's face twists in disgust. "What's her problem? I mean, she can't even say hi to me?"

Jenny rolls her eyes, ignoring the comment as she walks over to Ferris and pretends to check the appetizers—leaving Kate standing there alone with the champagne.

"Hey, I thought you said your new boyfriend was coming?" Ferris says as Jenny starts adding chips to the platter.

"Uh, yeah, I thought so too." She pauses. "We talked yesterday, and he said he was definitely coming. But I've been texting him all day, and I haven't heard back." She looks disappointed, but Jenny isn't one to make things about herself. Her attention quickly shifts to the other end of the table, where Christy is pouring water all over the food.

"Oh, no, no, no—we don't do that," Jenny says, hurrying over. She gently takes the water bottle from Christy's hands and starts scanning the room. Meanwhile, Christy runs over and grabs the entire chip bag, which knocks over the salsa, crashing onto the floor. Jenny rubs her forehead.

"Okay, I think we're done playing with the food," Ferris says, scanning the room. Christy looks up at him, then quickly ducks under the table. Jenny exhales sharply through her nose, her gaze shifting from Christy to the mess on the floor and back to Ferris. He runs a hand through his hair. "Uh, I'm gonna find Callum or Gretchen," he says before making a quick exit.

After a few minutes of searching, Ferris finally spots Callum in the basement, beer in hand, laughing with Gretchen and a group of friends.

"There you guys are!" Ferris exhales, forcing a smile as he approaches. "Can you guys get Christy upstairs?"

Gretchen just looks over at Ferris like he's interrupting. Callum, taking a long sip of his beer, finally asks, "Is there a problem?"

"She's kind of wreaking havoc on our food table."

Gretchen cuts in, "I'm sorry, she's a kid. What do you expect me to do?"

"I don't know, maybe just tell her not to do that?

"Callum, could you? I've had a long day with her."

Without missing a beat, Callum puts his beer down and heads upstairs with Ferris, leaving the buzz of conversation behind.

Sloan, doing her best to keep her mind off Ferris's mom, spends the next little while soaking in the warmth of her family and friends. She laughs at stories shared by her mom, finds comfort in the chatter with her close friends, and lets herself be distracted by the easy joy of those who truly care about her.

As the evening winds down, the last bites of appetizers are cleared away, and the announcement of dessert brings a sweet close to the meal. Soft music hums in the background as Ferris and

Sloan share a quiet moment, exchanging smiles while the last of the guests settle into the kitchen area.

Jenny steps up from her spot near the table, a glass in her hand. She taps it gently to catch everyone's attention, the room falling into a gentle hush.

"Hey, everyone," she begins, her voice warm and inviting. "I just want to take a moment to make a quick announcement." She scans the small crowd of family and friends, her gaze lingering on Sloan and Ferris. "We're here today to celebrate two truly incredible people, and I just want to thank you all for being here to share this moment with us."

She turns her attention to Sloan, a soft smile spreading across her face. "I feel so fortunate that my brother found someone as kind, intelligent, and driven as you. From the moment I met you, you've felt like a sister to me."

Sloan smiles, fighting back tears.

Jenny continues, her tone filled with warmth, "And Ferris, well, I didn't have much choice but to love you, but I guess I'm lucky for that, too. So, on behalf of everyone, I just want to say how excited we all are for this next step in your journey. Here's to celebrating your love."

Just then, sniffles can be heard to the side of the room. Sloan looks over to see Kate rubbing her nose profusely with a tissue.

Ted puts his arm around his wife and whispers something quietly that Sloan can't quite make out. Kate loudly replies, "It's my only son's engagement and I'm forbidden to even say anything!"

The people around her and across the room start to look with worry.

Ted, trying to lighten the mood, responds, "Aw Kate, no one said you can't say anything! Hey Jenny, Mom would like to say something." By now, everyone's attention is on Kate.

Kate, ready for her moment, chimes in, "Thank you, Ted. I would, so I—"

Ferris locks eyes with Jenny and shakes his head. "That actually won't be necessary, Mom."

Kate immediately slips into victim mode. "Excuse me, I will say a few words at my *son's* engagement party." Her tone shifts from passive-aggressive to forceful, and the crowd's eyes begin bouncing around from person to person like a game of ping pong.

Sloan, unable to bite her tongue any longer, steps forward and interrupts. "No, you will not. We are only going to have speeches from people that actually support us."

"I beg your pardon? I *support* you."

Ferris jumps in, trying to save the night. "Mom, can we not right now? Let's just carry on with the evening, please."

The unease in the room was growing heavier by the second. It clings to the air like humidity before a thunderstorm—thick and suffocating, impossible to ignore.

"No, you guys are just being downright rude. I only want to say a few words," Kate says, glancing around the room. She lets out a dramatic sigh before adding with a saccharine smile, "Is that really too much for little ol' me?" The expression is meant to soften her words, but everyone can see the manipulation behind it.

Suddenly, Sloan gets an idea. "You know what? It's fine. You want to make a speech, Kate? Go right ahead," she says with a sweet smile. Then, just loud enough for only Ferris beside her to hear, she murmurs, "Let everyone see what a monster she really is."

"Great, thank you, Sloan. I knew you'd come around," Kate says as she stands and makes her way next to Jenny. "I just want to say a few quick words, then you can all get back to enjoying your evening."

Jenny takes this as her cue to start quietly passing plates of desserts around the group.

Sloan straightens in her chair, her pulse quickening as Ferris rests a hand on her knee—both of them bracing for his mother to inevitably dig her own grave.

"You know, this has been a very difficult time for me as a mother," Kate begins, her voice carrying just the right touch of wounded sorrow. "He's my only son, you know, and I never imagined someone would come along and rip him from my arms so soon."

Sloan shifts in her seat, feeling Ferris's hand tighten slightly on her knee. He forces a polite smile, but the tension in his jaw betrays him. Around the room, guests exchange wary glances, the clinking of forks against dessert plates the only sound filling the awkward pause.

"And you know, it's hard to trust that he's making the right decision, but I've just learned to really shut my mouth and trust the process and hope that one day he can just, you know, figure it out on his own."

Sloan turns to Ferris, her brows knitting together in disbelief, her lips pressed into a thin line. She doesn't say a word, but the sharpness in her gaze says it all.

Ferris gritted his teeth. His mother had always been dramatic. But this? This was something else. He could feel Sloan tense beside him, waiting for him to say something. But his throat was dry, his heart hammering.

Saying this out loud would change things. It would mean finally drawing a line. He takes a slow breath and squares his shoulders.

"Alright, I think that's gonna be enough," he says, looking directly at Kate. He then turns to look at the rest of the guests, "Thank you, everyone, for coming—please grab some dessert and hang out as long as you'd like!"

"But wait, I'm not done!" Kate protests, lifting a hand, her voice rising over the chatter.

Ferris exhales, shaking his head. "I think we've had enough speeches for one night. People came to celebrate—not sit through a whole lecture."

At this point, Ted rises from his seat behind Kate and begins steering her toward the dessert table. She resists, planting her feet. With a few lingering gazes on her, she seizes the moment to make one last cutting remark.

"There you go, everyone. This is what happens when they meet the love of their life—Mom gets cut out," she snaps, her voice sharp and biting.

Ted, unfazed, casually plucks a brownie from the tray and leans in to murmur something low to Kate. She jerks away from his touch and storms toward the counter. With a dramatic huff, she snatches her purse, yanking it over her shoulder. Her heels stab into the floor with every step as she stomps toward the door, making sure everyone hears her exit. Ted offers a small, tired nod to the room before trailing behind her, dessert still in hand. The door clicks shut behind them, and with that, the energy in the room seems to finally release its grip.

For a moment, no one says anything.

Jenny exhales, shaking her head. "Well, that went about as well as expected."

Sloan blinks, still feeling the weight in the air—like static that hasn't quite cleared. "Did it?"

Ferris turns to her, taking her hands in his. "Hey. We made it through this. We'll make it through the wedding too."

She squeezes his fingers, exhaling slowly. "We better."

Part 3

Chapter 8

Jenny is sitting on the couch at home, scrolling through Instagram. Her thumb swipes absently, pausing only when a photo of Charlie pops up—another one of his posts, showing him out with friends, smiling, having a good time. The same Charlie who had stood her up, the one she had actually thought might be different.

She wonders what she ever saw in him. However, the answer comes quickly when she remembers that kiss in the rain.

She met Charlie at a bar a couple months back, the night she was out celebrating after passing her exam. He'd had dark brown stubble, worn a backward hat, and a jersey for some team she didn't recognize. From across the bar, he sent her a drink. She met his gaze and took a sip.

They spent the rest of the night deep in conversation. He asked her questions, listening when she talked, which made her feel giddy inside. Then, as they stepped outside, rain poured down. They were about to head in opposite directions when he stopped and said, *"If I don't do this now, I'm going to regret it."*

He'd traced a hand along Jenny's jawline before tilting her chin toward him, capturing her lips in a slow, deliberate kiss.

But it was bullshit. All of it.

She clicks on the picture, her eyes narrowing as she studies it. *So, he's doing just fine,* she thinks. He hasn't texted her in weeks—not since the day of the engagement party. That night, he seemed so interested, eager to see her again and meet her family. And then... nothing.

Just then, a call pops up on her screen. Her heart stops, thinking she accidentally clicked something on his profile.

But alas, it's just her mom.

Reluctantly, Jenny answers, but before she can say anything, Kate is already talking, "Jenny, I'm gonna need you to reach out to Sloan and get the names and addresses of people she wants invited to the shower."

"Names for the shower? What are you talking about?" She couldn't possibly be this dense.

"Her bridal shower. What do you think I mean, Jenny? If you're going to be her Maid of Honor, you need to know these things."

"Mom, I know what a bridal shower is. What I'm wondering is why *you* need those names?" She couldn't be serious. Did she actually think she was going to be a part of planning the shower after everything?

Kate pauses and Jenny can hear the annoyance in her voice. "So that I can get started on planning the shower and understand how many people to expect."

Okay, we're doing this. Jenny comes in abruptly, "Oh, that won't be necessary. I've already started planning with her mom."

"Sorry, what? Sloan's Mom? And you didn't tell me?" her voice dripped with self-pity. "Why would you guys exclude me?"

Jenny takes a long exhale. "If someone treated you horribly at every single event, would you want them around you? I don't really blame her. This is supposed to be an exciting time and you're killing the vibe." She takes her phone off her ear, puts her mom on speaker, and continues to scroll. She knows this will be an ongoing debate where her mom just listens to respond...never to actually listen and understand.

"Okay well, what do I need to do to have it at my house? I have the perfect house for hosting," she starts to talk faster like she's a kid trying to barter for more dessert after dinner.

"Nothing, you've done enough," Jenny starts to respond like she's pre-programmed, having lost the energy to waste time explaining to her mother. "Sloan's Mom is going to host the party at her house, and we put the deposit down on the catering this week, so it's all set."

"Were you talking about me earlier? When you said if someone treated you horribly, would you want them around?" her mom asks.

Jenny lets out a dry laugh. "What gave it away?"

"The way I've been treating Sloan lately? This is all an over-exaggeration. I am just looking out for Ferris. I don't want him to make a huge mistake. Can you blame me?"

"Mom, Ferris obviously loves Sloan, so I don't know how you can't understand that this is not normal behavior," Jenny takes a moment, knowing this next part might sting. "He's a grown man, he doesn't need his mommy to protect him." She stands up, pacing around the room, her phone still on speaker, lying on the table. She glances over at the clock, noticing how late it's getting.

Kate scoffs loudly and dramatically enough for Ted to veer over from the other room. "Okay, tell me, what have I done that was so terrible to Sloan?"

Jenny rummages through the fridge, snacking on random things before realizing there's a pause. Her mom is genuinely asking…not just rhetorically. Perfect, Jenny's been ready for this. Maybe it was the anger at Charlie coming out, maybe the annoyance of being the peacekeeper of the family, or maybe it was because she simply had enough, but she came in hot, and she didn't care.

"Where do you want me to start, Mom? Let's see… when they started dating, you cried because you wouldn't get to spend his birthday alone with him anymore. When Ferris invited her to a family holiday for the first time, you asked why she wasn't with her own family."

Jenny paces the living room, her free hand gesturing in frustration as she picks the phone back up to her ear. On the other end, her mom exhales sharply, the sound crackling through the speaker like she's barely holding back her own outburst.

"You constantly criticize the way she dresses, asking who she's trying to impress. You tried to talk Ferris out of proposing. Then, you attempted to crash their special vacation. You showed up to the engagement party even after they asked you not to. And when you did, you made a speech tearing Sloan down the entire time."

Jenny stops, pressing a hand to her forehead, forcing herself to take a breath. "Should I keep going?" For a brief moment, she wonders if should have backed down a little—but the thought vanishes the second her mom speaks.

"Wow. I guess after everything I've done for you guys, I'm just a horrible person, and no one should be around me."

Jenny doesn't take the bait. She knows exactly what her mom is doing—playing the victim, hoping to make her feel guilty, to make her back down. But she won't.

"I have nothing to say," Jenny finally replies, her voice steady. "I just think you need to take a long look in the mirror and see how you've treated other people. I've gotta go, Mom." And with that, she hangs up the phone.

Jenny exhales sharply, tossing her phone onto the couch beside her. Her heart is still racing, but whether it's from the argument or something else, she isn't sure.

Her gaze drifts back to the screen, to the photo of Charlie still open on Instagram. Maybe she wasn't just mad at her mom—maybe she was pissed at him too, at the way people take and take, never thinking about how their actions affect others. Without hesitating, she taps his profile, hovers for a second, then blocks him.

Chapter 9

Kate stands in front of her bathroom mirror, smoothing the lines of her blouse with careful precision. The morning light filters through the window, casting a soft glow on the vanity as she reaches for her lipstick—a bright red, bold and intentional. She applies it slowly, pressing her lips together before giving herself one last look.

She walks over to the nightstand, grabs her glasses, and wipes the lenses clean before slipping them on. Taking a measured breath, she straightens her shoulders as she heads to the kitchen. This call needs to go right. It has to. With a practiced calm, she picks up her phone, scrolling through her contacts until she lands on the name Virginia Bartels—Sloan's mother.

A slight hesitation, just for a moment—then, she clicks the green button to dial. It rings and rings, Kate growing impatient as she taps the counter with her long merlot-colored fingernails.

Suddenly, the call connects. There's a pause before a quiet, "Hello?"

Kate enthusiastically and calmly answers back, "Hi, is this Virginia? This is Kate Hayes, Ferris's Mom."

"Yes, this is Virginia," her response was polite but cold. "What can I do for you, Kate?"

"Well, I just got off the phone with my daughter—you know, Jenny—and she mentioned that you all have started planning Ferris and Sloan's bridal shower. How exciting!"

The thing was, Kate *was* excited—well, maybe that wasn't the right word. Enthusiastic, perhaps, but in a way that felt more about appearances than genuine joy. She always knew Ferris would get married someday, but not to someone like Sloan. Not now.

It's not that she *dislikes* Sloan; she just doesn't think she's the right fit for Ferris. He's always been so ambitious and so involved with his family, but now his priorities are shifting. She doesn't want him to *settle*—not when he deserves so much more.

Virginia stays silent as Kate steamrolls the conversation. Her pen scrapes against the notepad on her desk at work, each stroke pressing harder and harder as she listens. She's only met Kate a handful of times, and there's never been a real relationship between them. But she's heard the way Kate talks to her daughter, the little comments, the passive-aggressive jabs.

This wasn't a call about support. It was a call about *control*.

Kate continues, oblivious. "I would love to help you guys out with that. You know, I *love* hosting. I've thrown so many parties in my day—"

Virginia glances at her phone. *Ten minutes.* Ten full minutes of Kate rambling without a single pause for her to speak.

She cuts in, sharp and deliberate. "I'm gonna stop you right there. *Karen*, was it?"

Kate clears her throat, "Kate."

Virginia continues, "All right, Kate, well, listen here. I'm also really good at hosting parties, and I'm also really good at keeping good boundaries with people that don't treat my daughter, or myself, with respect." She sits up at her desk, wondering if that was too direct. She's not normally confrontational, but sometimes Mama Bear comes out and you can't control it.

Kate is confused, "Oh, well, I hardly know you. How am I not treating you with respect?"

Virginia is sick of the front, sick of the games. "Because when you disrespect my daughter, who has been nothing but nice to you over the last almost three years now, you are disrespecting me too."

Kate is as white as a ghost, but her cheeks burn hot. A prickling heat crawls up her neck as the words settle, sharp and unshakable. Her mouth opens, but nothing comes out—just a shaky breath. She's *never* been spoken to like that before.

"Oh, suddenly you're speechless? Funny, you're never speechless around Sloan. You constantly put her down, making her feel like she's not good enough."

"I'm not speechless," Kate snaps, though her voice wavers. "I'm just... trying to figure out what to say here. I mean, I just want what's best for my son. Can you blame me for being protective?"

"And I want what's best for my daughter. Can you blame *me* for being protective when someone treats her this way?" Virginia exhales sharply. She finally *gets it*. Sloan has told her about these conversations for years but experiencing it firsthand is something else entirely. This woman is *insufferable*—trapped in her own web of excuses, always the victim, never pausing to consider anyone else's perspective.

"I'm supporting her now, aren't I?"

Virginia's assistant pops around the corner, eyes wide, like he's trying to make sure everything's okay. Virginia gives a slight smile and thumbs up to show she's fine, just dealing with a situation. "Are you? Or are you just trying to make yourself look good in front of everybody now?"

That one hurts. "No, of course not. It was just initially hard for me to understand why they wanted to rush into marriage. I mean, I hardly know Sloan."

Virginia rolls her eyes. The argument is exhausting, they've been together almost three years—she'd hardly call that rushing. "Well, yeah, lucky for Sloan, Ferris is very smart, and he can speak for himself."

Kate, now looking in a mirror, smiles to herself, "Yes, he can. I raised a smart boy."

"Okay, but do you see how you're contradicting yourself?" Virginia leans forward, her tone firm but even. "You say you raised a smart boy, yet you're constantly in his ear, trying to steer him toward decisions that suit *you* better."

Kate's forced smile fades, her lips pressing into a thin line. She exhales sharply through her nose and walks out to her living room, her heels clicking against the hardwood.

Virginia doesn't let up. "I'm sorry if this seems harsh, but after years of my daughter coming home from your house in tears because of something you said, I've had it." Her pulse quickens, her grip tightening around the edge of the table. "This is supposed to be one of the happiest times in her life, and instead, she's constantly on edge, waiting for the next thing you're going to pull. I won't let you ruin it."

When she finally speaks, Kate's voice is small, almost fragile—"I don't want to ruin it."

Virginia exhales, glancing at her computer screen. A meeting starts in five minutes. "Great. Then if you actually want to make things better and move forward, you're going to need to apologize to Sloan."

Kate hesitates before mumbling, "What should I say?"

Virginia's patience is thinning. "If I have to tell a grown woman how to apologize, we might as well cut our losses now."

Kate asks one final time about helping with the shower. Virginia doesn't hesitate. "We won't be needing your help," she says firmly. "And unless you can apologize to Sloan, you might want to make other arrangements for that day, because we won't be wanting to see you."

With that, she ends the call.

Chapter 10

Two weeks pass in a blur, but the tension lingers.

Kate sits at her dining table, tapping her nails against the wood, her phone lying face-up in front of her. The screen is dark, but she knows exactly what she needs to do.

She exhales sharply, smoothing down the front of her blouse as if that alone could steady her. The house is quiet—too quiet. She's rehearsed this conversation a dozen times, yet her throat still feels tight.

This call has to go well.

She gets up to grab her phone, but before dialing, she tries to practice what she's going to say. She remembers speech class in high school, where they used to tell students to practice in front of a mirror. So, she walks over to the one in the foyer, looks at herself, takes a deep breath, and starts.

"Hey, Sloan, this is Kate. I just want to say I'm sorry."

The words feel foreign on her tongue, unnatural, like they don't belong to her. She tries again.

"I'm sorry."

She pauses, watching her reflection as her mouth forms the word, testing how it sounds. Then she continues, pushing forward.

"I talked to your mom. I, as a mother... you know, Ferris is... okay, so, Sloan, we got off on the wrong foot."

The words stumble out, tangled and unsure, even in practice. She's never had to do this before—apologize, especially for something she doesn't even think she did wrong. She exhales sharply, straightening her posture.

Whatever. I just need to get this over with.

She grabs her phone, her fingers hovering over the screen before finally pressing the dial button.

***

Sloan rinses off the last dish, shaking off the excess water before setting it on the drying rack. Behind her, Ferris grabs the bottle of wine from the counter and pours a generous splash into her glass.

"Here," he says, setting it beside her with a small smile. "Least I can do since you're handling dishes."

Sloan smirks. "Oh, wow, look at you."

Ferris chuckles, taking his own glass and heading toward the couch. He sinks into the cushions, stretching his legs out with a satisfied sigh. Sloan walks over to join him and they snuggle in together as Ferris gives her a kiss on her forehead.

Just as Sloan leans forward to reach for her glass, her phone vibrates on the table next to her. She glances down and immediately tenses.

Kate.

Her stomach knots. She exhales slowly, pressing her lips together before setting the wine down, suddenly not as interested in drinking it.

Ferris, noticing her hesitation, frowns. "Who is it?"

Wordlessly, she tilts the screen toward him. His easygoing expression shifts.

"You gonna answer?" he asks carefully.

Sloan stares at the name flashing on the screen. "I don't know," she admits. "I really don't feel like talking to her right now."

Ferris shrugs. "You don't have to. You absolutely do not need to answer."

Sloan smirks. "Yeah—I'm not going to." She presses decline and sets her phone back on the table, smiling to herself. Picking up her wine glass, she takes a long, slow sip. With a satisfied sigh, she sinks into the couch beside Ferris.

He grabs the remote, ready to put on a movie, when his own phone lights up. "Great. Now she's calling me." He shoots Sloan a look before glancing back at the screen, debating.

Sloan raises an eyebrow, her expression clear—*Do what you want, but don't involve me.*

Ferris exhales. "I'm just gonna answer. Maybe something happened." He swipes to pick up the call. "Hey, Mom. What's going on?"

Kate's voice comes through immediately, slightly breathless. "Ferris, I'm so glad you answered." There's a short pause and Ferris instantly regrets answering. "Look, are you with Sloan? I need to talk to her." Sloan's eyes grow wide, overhearing Kate. She silently mouths, "I'm not here," exaggerating each word as she motions at Ferris.

"Uh... no, sorry, she just ran out. What's going on?"

"Well, look, I really need to talk to her, so when she gets back, um, can you have her give me a call?"

Sloan sits there looking over at Ferris shaking her head. There's no way she will be calling Kate back.

Ferris puts his hand to his forehead, "What is it regarding, Mom?"

"Well, I just got off the phone with her mom and we were talking about her wedding shower...your guy's wedding shower, and I would really like to be a part of it," she seems to be nervous as she starts to ramble, "It's also been brought to my attention that I've made Sloan upset more times than I can count and I want to right my wrongs."

Sloan silently laughs beside him, feeling the ridiculousness of it all.

Ferris glances over at her. He understands why she finds this whole thing comical—how Kate's sudden shift feels more like a performance than a breakthrough—but a small part of him still holds out hope that his mom is actually trying.

"Wow. It's finally gotten through to you how awful you've been to Sloan over the years?" Kate lets out a soft gasp, her hand briefly fluttering near her chest.

"Okay, I didn't say awful," she snaps quickly. "I just said... maybe there were times I didn't realize I wasn't being very kind to her." Her eyes dart around the room like she's searching for words that could make the truth sound less harsh. "But truth be told," she adds, her voice dipping into something that almost sounds sincere, "I just don't want you waking up one day and realizing... you picked the wrong person."

Ferris holds the phone slightly away from his ear, side-eyeing Sloan, who is now nervously swirling the last bit of wine in her glass. She doesn't say anything, but the smirk tugging at the corner of her lips says enough—she doesn't believe a word of it. Ferris exhales, dragging a hand through his hair before reaching out to squeeze Sloan's hand.

"Okay, well, I'm going to be honest with you, Mom. Sloan doesn't want to talk to you right now."

Kate makes a noise of protest, but Ferris continues. "I think you might just need to give her some space."

Kate's voice sharpens, teetering on desperation. "But Virginia said I can't come to the shower unless I apologize. And if I can't apologize, how am I supposed to help put it together?" She starts to panic, not because she actually cares about planning the shower, but because she feels the line in the sand being drawn thicker now. The realization that she might actually be excluded from something so *important* is settling in, and it stings. Ferris is slipping away, her sense of control slipping with him.

Ferris sighs, pressing his thumb and forefinger into his temple. "Maybe it's best if you let them handle the shower, and you just come as a guest."

Kate scoffs, her voice rising with indignation. "*Just* come as a guest? But I'm your *mother!* The mother of the groom!" She's yelling now.

Sloan closes her eyes for a moment, willing Ferris to end the conversation. He's doing a great job standing up for her, and she appreciates it, but it's *exhausting* to keep going in circles with this woman. The weight of it, the years of forced tolerance, sit heavy on her shoulders.

Ferris leans forward, rubbing his forehead. "Yeah, well, you kind of ruined that when you showed up to the engagement party you were *explicitly* asked not to attend, and then insisted on making a speech." He glances over at Sloan and winks, softening the edge in his voice. "So let me talk to Sloan when she gets home," he says, grinning at her. "And I'll see if she agrees to let you come to the shower—if and only if you promise not to say anything rude to her."

Kate takes a sharp inhale—the kind that burns in her lungs—but she doesn't argue. She *can't* argue. She mumbles a quick goodbye, and the line goes dead.

Ferris exhales hard, tossing his phone onto the coffee table like it's physically weighed down by his mother's words. He stares blankly across the room, proud of himself—but also gutted. The firmer his boundaries get, the more he wonders if he's starting to lose her for good.

Sloan leans forward to top off her wine, then sinks back into the couch, one knee tucked to her chest.

Later that night, as she lies awake in bed, Sloan turns the question over in her mind. She knew Ferris would support her either way, but would he quietly resent her if she ultimately said his mother couldn't come?

And what would their lives look like down the line, maneuvering all of that? Torn between keeping the peace and protecting her sanity, Sloan makes a decision: she would let Kate come to the shower—as a guest. That was it. No planning, no input, no sense of control. If she had to spend any more time around Kate than necessary, she was going to snap.

This was her boundary, and Kate was going to have to live with it.

The thing was, she *loved* Ferris. A lot. But sometimes, she questioned if it was all worth it. She had never felt such indirect hatred from someone her whole life and for no particular reason. She was a good partner to Ferris. She was a good person. She worked hard.

What more did Kate want?

The stress of dealing with her constant shenanigans was becoming too much to handle, and it was starting to take a toll. Sloan sighed, rolling onto her side and staring up at the dark ceiling.

She had made her decision. She just hoped it was the right one.

Chapter 11

Two months pass, and the day of the wedding shower arrives. Jenny loads up her car and heads to Virginia's house to start setting up. As she steps onto the porch, the door swings open before she can knock.

"Hi, Jenny! Come on in," Virginia greets her with a warm smile. Her sleek black hair frames her face, and the forest green dress she's wearing—with delicate embroidery at the collar and wrists—adds to her natural grace.

Stepping inside, Jenny is enveloped in a warmth she isn't used to. Unlike the pristine, museum-like home she grew up in, this house feels lived-in—inviting. Framed photos line the walls, capturing years of laughter, milestones, and everyday moments. A stack of books sits casually on the coffee table as if someone had just set them down mid-read. Plush couches are draped with a patchwork of throw blankets, each one seemingly collected over years of holidays and family gatherings.

Soft golden light spills through the windows, casting a cozy glow. The air is rich with something sweet and familiar—cinnamon, maybe vanilla. It smells like home.

Jenny exhales, feeling something unfamiliar settle in her chest—something like longing. She had spent her life tiptoeing through perfectly arranged but lifeless spaces. But here, in Sloan's mom's home, she feels something else entirely.

"Here, let me help you," Virginia reaches out to grab one of the boxes in Jenny's arms and leads her back through the house. "I hope you found it okay!"

"I did! Thanks again for hosting. You really have a beautiful home," Jenny replies, still admiring the feeling inside her chest.

Virginia doesn't say anything, just smiles to herself as they arrive at the kitchen and set the items on the counter. They start chatting about the plan for the day as they begin to place items around the house.

***

Upstairs in her childhood bedroom, Sloan puts the final touches on her look. If it were up to her, she'd be downstairs helping set up, but Jenny and her mom insisted on surprising her and Ferris.

Stress had been a constant since the engagement. Juggling her final semester of student teaching, wedding planning, and now everything with Kate, this was far from the wedded bliss she'd once imagined. She had never expected to deal with a future in-law who felt more like an adversary.

On the surface, Sloan projected confidence in keeping Kate out of the planning, but inside, it gnawed at her. She knew Kate didn't deserve to be involved, but setting firm boundaries had never come naturally to her. She had grown up in a supportive family—arguments happened, of course, but outright jealousy and malice were foreign concepts. Kate's resentment was something entirely different, and it unsettled her more than she wanted to admit.

Sloan swipes on the last coat of mascara, then steps to the closet to slip into her dress. It struck the perfect balance—chic and playful, yet unmistakably bridal. The soft white fabric skims just above her knees, with delicate lace tracing the hem and sleeves. A subtle sweetheart neckline frames her collarbones, while the cinched waist accentuates her figure before flaring into a gentle A-line. Romantic yet modern, simple yet stunning—it was made for celebrating.

Ferris, on the other hand, was getting ready in Sloan's brother's room. Her brother was a few years younger and away at college, so he wouldn't be around for the weekend. Ferris kept it business casual—navy pants, a cream button-down, and a navy suit jacket, skipping the tie for a more modern look.

Stepping into the hall bathroom to style his hair, he catches Sloan's reflection in the mirror and freezes. This was the woman he would soon get to call his wife. Her caramel skin glowed under the soft lighting, a stunning contrast against the white lace of her dress.

"Well, hello, I don't believe we've met," he teases, still stunned by her beauty.

Sloan glances over, playfully rolling her eyes. "We haven't, but you better get out of here before my fiancé sees you," she says with a laugh, knowing full well that role-playing wasn't really her thing.

"Your fiancé, huh? He must be one lucky guy." Ferris smirks, leaning in to press a kiss to her cheek.

Sloan quickly turns her head, meeting his lips instead. In an instant, his arms wrap around her waist, pulling her closer. She slides her fingers through his hair, and for a brief moment, they toy with the idea of taking it further—until the creak of the stairs snaps them back to reality.

"You guys ready? We're all set—" Jenny stops short with a small shriek, dramatically covering her eyes. "Really, guys? In your mother's home?" She glances directly at Sloan at the last part.

Ferris laughs, shaking his head as he pulls Sloan in closer. "Not our fault you walked up here without announcing yourself."

"Alright, next time I'll be sure to be louder," Jenny teases, turning to head back down the stairs. "Anyways, we're all done setting up downstairs, so whenever you two are ready, feel free to join...if you aren't too busy." She rolls her eyes.

"Thanks, Jenny. We'll be down in a minute," Sloan replies, playfully smacking Ferris's shoulder.

Ferris and Sloan decide to stay upstairs a little longer to have some time alone before things get too hectic. As family and friends start to arrive, the house fills with the sounds of chatter and laughter.

When they finally make their way downstairs, the smell of pasta sauce fills the air, instantly making them both hungry. Jenny, noticing them coming down, takes the opportunity to throw the spotlight on them. "Everyone, our honorary guests have arrived!"

At the bottom of the stairs, Sloan's mom, Virginia, greets them both with a warm hug and glasses of champagne. "You two are so loved. Just look at this room already starting to fill up with your fans!" She winks and quickly moves on to greet another guest at the door.

Ferris and Sloan steal a quiet moment with each other, soaking it all in. The house is decorated with simple, refined charm—understated, yet undeniably beautiful. Soft white linens drape over the tables, accented by delicate floral arrangements in shades of sage and ivory. Candles flicker gently, casting a warm, inviting glow across the room. String lights weave through the space, adding just the right touch of romance without feeling overdone. A tasteful balloon arch frames the entryway, while handwritten signs and thoughtful details give everything a personal, intimate feel. It's the kind of décor that doesn't scream for attention but quietly elevates the moment, making the space feel both special and welcoming.

They spend the next half an hour circulating, greeting guests, and responding to what seems like a rehearsed set of questions:
"Let me see your ring! Ah, Ferris, you did so good!"
"Are you ready for the big day?"
"How's wedding planning going?"

Virginia makes an announcement that lunch is ready, so all of the guests start making their way to the buffet line to fill their plates. The room quickly fills with the smell of butter, garlic, and pasta sauce. As everyone starts to head to the tables to settle down, Sloan and Ferris can't help but notice that Kate is nowhere to be found, although they don't feel the need to mention it or say anything about it to each other.

Just as this is happening, Kate pulls up in front of the house in her white Cadillac Escalade. "Hopefully they won't mind that we're a little late," she says, knowing that this was her plan all along. Being kept out of planning your son's wedding shower was rude enough, so she needed to make a grand entrance to make up for it.

Kate steps out of the Escalade with practiced elegance, moving slowly and deliberately, as if the world has no choice but to wait for her. She swings one leg out first, her designer heel touching the pavement with precision before she shifts her weight and gracefully rises from the seat. She then pulls both sides of her white and grey fur coat together to fasten the button before walking around to the back of her car to grab her gift and then continuing to walk up to the house. Along with her, two friends get out of the car. As she makes her way up to the door, the shimmering fabric of her ivory dress catches the light as she smooths it down, her movements unhurried, effortlessly commanding attention.

"Are you sure it's okay we came with you?" the first friend, Julie, asks.

"Absolutely! They'll just squeeze you in," Kate says without pause, "Honestly, I'm a little embarrassed you never received your invitation."

"Wow, I can't believe your Ferris is getting married," the second friend, Cindy, says, "I can't wait to meet his wife. She's got the best future mother-in-law."

Kate laughs and smiles widely to herself as she reaches the front step and opens the door. She's surprised when no one is there to greet her, although she hears chatter throughout the house. Kate takes a slow glance around, her lips pressing into a thin line. Of all places, Virginia had insisted on hosting here? Her house would have been way better.

As she reaches the kitchen, Ferris spots her from across the room and immediately starts making his way over. Even with everything going on, he still feels caught at a crossroad—torn between letting her be and feeling responsible for her every move.

"Mom, you're here," he pauses, trying not to sound too surprised, "And with a couple friends."

Kate ignores Ferris's comment. She smiles at him and quickly gives him a hug and peck on the cheek before turning back to her friends, "Ladies, you remember my son Ferris, and his beautiful bride-to-be is around here somewhere." She turns back to Ferris while still talking to her friends, "You'll see her. She's gorgeous."

The first time Kate is complementing Sloan and she's not even here to see it for herself. Ferris knows this is his mom trying to make it seem like she's a great mother-in-law, but he can see through it. He's just not sure her friends can.

Jenny notices them talking at the front and hurries to intervene as soon as possible. She doesn't want her mom to cause any unwanted stress on the future bride and groom. "Hey, Mom! Glad you made it," she pauses, noticing her outfit, "You know it started at noon, right?"

"I know," Kate quickly replies, looking the other way.

"Okay, well it's almost twelve-thirty, and it's not like you to get somewhere late."

"I know where I'm not wanted."

Jenny has to stop her eyes from rolling. "Right. Okay, so, um, who did you bring with you? You didn't mention you were bringing anyone with you when you RSVP'd."

"Well, I called Julie and Cindy last week to see if they wanted a carpool today and, can you believe it—neither of them got the invitation! So, I said, just come along with me and we'll just squeeze them in. I'm sure it's not a big deal, right?"

"Well, I'm sure in the grand scheme of things it's not a big deal, but we have everything set up, and I have the exact number of chairs for everyone who RSVPed. So, I'm sorry, but you can't just bring people without telling me."

Kate lightly touches Jenny's jawline, her smile saccharine. "Oh, Jenny, I'm sorry, but these are two of my oldest friends, and you didn't even ask me for a guest list," She glances around the room, feigning curiosity. "Now, where are Sloan and her mom? I'd love to say hi." She looks directly at Ferris and winks at her friends, who are starting to look slightly uncomfortable.

Ferris notices Sloan looking over, and as they lock eyes, he nervously says, "Hey honey, wanna come over here?"

Sloan hesitantly rises from her seat, smoothing down her dress as she starts toward Ferris and Kate. But before she can take another step, Virginia notices and places a hand on Sloan's arm, stopping her in her tracks. "Let me." Without waiting for a response, she steps forward, her posture poised and unwavering as she heads straight for Kate.

Chapter 12

"Karen, you made it!" Virginia says as she approaches closer.

"It's Kate."

"Sure, sure. Anyway, there may have been some confusion, so let me clarify. You were invited as a guest, and you RSVPed for one. Yet, you brought two extra people." Virginia's tone remains polite, but firm. "Now, as the Mother of the Bride, I'll do my best to make room for them— *if* you behave as a Mother of the Groom should." She takes a deliberate step closer, lowering her voice just enough for only Kate to hear. "That means no rude comments, no backhanded remarks, and absolutely no embarrassing my daughter today. Are we clear?"

Kate glances at her friends, shifting uncomfortably, her confidence wavering under Virginia's stare. Then, with a forced laugh, she waves a dismissive hand. "Oh, Virginia, you crack me up." Her voice is light, but there's a nervous edge to it.

Without missing a beat, she turns to Sloan and her friends, reclaiming control of the moment. "Julie, Cindy, I want you to meet my future daughter-in-law." She pauses just long enough to glance at Virginia as if silently pleading innocence. "This is Sloan... and her mother."

They exchange quiet hellos, and Sloan offers a polite smile. "Thank you for coming," she says, her tone gracious but reserved.

Virginia doesn't miss a beat. "Kate, I wasn't joking." She raises an eyebrow, her expression unwavering.

Kate's eyes widen slightly before she turns to her friends. "Girls, go ahead and head in. I'll be in shortly." Then, with a smirk, she pivots back to Virginia. "My friends here just spent a *lot* of money on gifts for your daughter. So, unless you'd like them to walk right back out with those gifts, I suggest you find two more seats," she says, her voice low and pointed.

Virginia barely blinks. "You might be all about money and gifts, but that's not my daughter. She couldn't care less about two presents from people she doesn't even know."

Sloan watches them go back and forth like a tennis match, realizing this is eating away at the celebration. With a deep breath, she gently places a hand on her mom's arm. "Mom, while I *do* agree that I couldn't care less about the gifts, this is already pulling focus from the event. I just want to enjoy today. Can we agree to disagree, get along, and move on?"

Virginia immediately snaps out of it, realizing she let Kate get the best of her again. She puts her hand on Sloan's. "Oh my gosh, you're right honey. I'm so sorry! I don't want to ruin your day. I just get into mama bear mode when someone tries to hurt my daughter," she looks directly at Kate one last time before guiding Sloan back into the main room.

Kate joins her friends in the main room, and they grab food. Virginia manages to squeeze them in at a table, sacrificing her own seat. As the host, she figures she didn't really need one—plus, she wants to keep an eye on things to make sure there isn't any funny business.

Over lunch, they play a few typical shower games. Once dessert is served, Virginia stands to announce it's time for gifts. Jenny moves two chairs to the front of the room for Ferris and Sloan, and guests angle their seats toward them to watch.

Kate wastes no time. She grabs her chair and heads straight for the front. "Mother of the Groom here!" she calls out, her voice carrying over the chatter. She plants herself in the front row, just a couple of feet from Sloan, who instantly feels her cheeks flush, a pit forming in her stomach.

Jenny, standing off to the side, orchestrates the gift-giving. She eyes Kate's proximity and says, "Mom, can you scoot back a little? You're practically on Sloan's lap."

Kate sighs but stands to nudge her chair back a couple of inches. "What's wrong with that?" she jokes, turning to grin at the guests behind her like she's onstage. Then, as if suddenly remembering something, she steps toward Jenny and points. "Give them that gold one over there! It's mine. They *need* to open mine first."

Jenny exhales sharply, lowering her voice. "Mom, please. They'll get to yours, I promise."

Kate clicks her tongue and flops back into her seat. "Sorry, I'm just excited. Can you blame me?" She flashes another wide smile at the crowd, clearly playing to her audience.

After Ferris and Sloan finish opening most of their gifts—amid plenty of *oohs* and *ahhs* from the group—Jenny finally grabs Kate's and sets it in front of them. "Wow, this is heavy."

Kate leans forward eagerly. "It's the bookshelf you wanted... well, one of them. The other is still at home. Ferris, you'll have to come pick it up." Then, as if realizing something, she stands up and covers her mouth. "Oops! Sorry, I didn't mean to spoil it. I just got so excited." She turns around, winking at her friends behind her.

Sloan starts unwrapping the gift while Kate continues, barely able to contain herself. "But open the drawer—there's a special surprise in there."

Sloan forces a small, polite smile at Kate. She hesitantly opens the drawer, half-expecting something to jump out. Instead, she finds a stack of books and pulls them out for everyone to see, "Okay, it looks like a couple of books." One of the guests yells out, "What books?" Sloan hesitates, scanning the covers before reading aloud, "Uh, 'From Miss to Mrs.: Refining Yourself for Marriage'", she swallows, "'When You Marry the Family: How to Respect Your Husband's Parents.'"

Ferris picks up the last book, reading the title slowly: 'What Happens After the Happily Ever After'—though it comes out more like a question. Sloan looks over at Ferris and then back at Kate who is now beaming in front of her, hands clasped by her face.

"I saw these at the thrift store, and I couldn't help but buy them. I think they'll be really helpful in the next chapter of your relationship-"

Ferris cuts in, "All right, well I think that's it, everybody." He says *'everybody'*, but he's looking directly at his mom, "Thank you all for coming. It really means a lot to have you here celebrating with us." He puts his arm around Sloan's back and leans in to kiss her. At the same time, Kate moves back by her friends at the table behind her and starts laughing.

Sloan kisses him back and whispers, "Well, that was embarrassing."

But more than that—it was a warning shot. As she stood there, smiling through it, her stomach twisted. *Is this what the rest of her life would look like? Humiliations softened by Ferris's arm around her? Apologies made with his eyes while his mom laughed behind her back?*

She hated the thought, but it was creeping in: *Was it time to walk away now... or was she really prepared to live like this forever?*

Ferris gently cups her face and looks into her eyes, "I'm sorry that happened. I should have stopped it sooner," he squeezes her hand as he starts to walk back into the group, "I'll tell you one thing though, my mom has never gone thrift shopping a day in her life, she bought those intentionally."

"Yeah, I don't even know what to say at this point," Sloan replies quietly.

Jenny walks up behind them and announces to everyone there's more dessert and favors if they would like to take some on the way out, thanking them again for coming. She then leans in to Sloan and her brother to let them know she's put some dessert aside for them and will grab some friends to help load up the gifts in the car.

They thank Jenny again for putting everything together as friends and family start finding their way over to say their goodbyes. They see Kate making small talk with those around her like she's a host, and when she starts gesturing over to them, Sloan decides that's enough.

She turns to Ferris, who hasn't left her side. "Look I've been friendly, and I've held my composure most of the day, but I don't think I can do it much longer. If your mom comes over here I might lose control. I'm going to say some quick thank yous, get some boxes in the car, and excuse myself from her until she's gone."

Ferris doesn't even try to convince her; he knows she's already dealt with enough. They say goodbye to everyone around them and as Kate gets closer, Sloan does as she said and heads out the door.

"Where did Sloan go?" she looks around frantically, "I was hoping she could tell me the plan for the bachelorette party."

Ferris looks at her with confused eyes. "What?"

"The bachelorette party—it's enough that I wasn't included in the wedding shower, and I hear these days women invite their mothers to it."

Ferris ignores everything his mother just said and completes the conversation with, "Sloan is busy helping her mom with something."

"Wow, that's awfully rude when so many people came here and took time out of their days to support her." She shoots an almost apologetic glance at her friends.

Ferris starts walking her towards the door and says, "Well, she said goodbye to everyone she invited and everyone she wanted here."

Kate takes a deep breath and squints, looking out behind him. Jenny walks over to the front door where they are standing. "Heading out, Mom?"

"Yes. Apparently, I'm not wanted here any longer and I've caused quite the problem, so much that my own future daughter-in-law can't even say goodbye to me." Jenny throws a look at her that makes her continue, "I know, I know…she's a busy bride! I know my place, don't gotta tell me twice."

"Apparently, we do, and a third and a fourth time. So, let me tell you again, next time, don't get the bride books as a passive-aggressive way of telling her you're unhappy with their relationship."

Kate waves a hand, ignoring Jenny's comment, "Well we're off to drinks at the Chateau! This was all amazing. You did a great job, Jenny," she says proudly. She walks out onto the front porch and starts to head to her car, but before she gets in, she turns around to yell, "I'll talk to you soon about the bachelorette party! Can't wait!"

Jenny stands there, stunned.

Upstairs, Sloan sits motionless on the edge of the bed, still in her dress, the soft fabric wrinkled beneath her hands. From upstairs, she could hear Kate's voice float through the open windows—cheerful, performative, and completely unaffected by the damage she'd caused.

Sloan's heart thuds in her chest. She hadn't even made it to the end of her own shower—*again*—because Kate had made it unbearable. From the snide comments to the underhanded gifts, it was like death by a thousand cuts. And even with Ferris's support, the constant emotional clean-up was wearing her down.

This wasn't just another ruined event. This was a pattern.

And if things were already this hard now... *what would their wedding day even look like?*

She blinks back tears, staring out the window as Kate's laughter fades into the night. For the first time, Sloan isn't wondering if she can handle Kate.

She is wondering if she can still walk down the aisle at all.

Part 4

Chapter 13

Ferris and Sloan had been ticking off wedding tasks for weeks now. The endless list of to-dos became their shared routine—selecting flowers, choosing a venue, and finally, sending out invitations. The RSVPs had begun trickling in, but there was still so much left to do.

In the midst of all the planning, Ferris has his own world to manage. As a project manager at a tech firm, his days are filled with tight deadlines, budget meetings, and coordinating teams to meet project milestones. Right now, he was hunched over his laptop in his home office, reviewing a series of reports and fielding calls from his team. A long day of problem-solving and logistics was no different than his typical workload, but the looming wedding and dealing with his family, well, mother, kept tugging at his mind.

Sloan, fresh off another busy day of student teaching, walks through the door, the familiar sound of the keys in the lock signaling the end of her day. She hangs her bag on the coat rack and kicks off her shoes. She yells out a "Hi hunny!" not realizing Ferris has his noise-cancelling headphones on.

She had grabbed the mail on her way in, and after setting down her things, she flips through the envelopes—freezing at the sight of an RSVP card from Callum and Gretchen. With only a week left before the RSVP deadline, she was surprised he hadn't sent it sooner. Things had been a little off since the engagement party. He used to stop by their house multiple times a week, but ever since he started dating Gretchen, he'd seemed less and less interested in being around.

Sloan pulls the card from the envelope and studies it, her fingers momentarily trembling before she sets it on the pile with a soft sigh. Realizing she hadn't heard Ferris reply when she got home, she wanders toward his office, leaning against the doorway with a big smile and a little wave.

Ferris glances up, quickly tugging off his headphones and setting them on the desk. "Hey, babe. How was school today?"

Sloan makes the face that only the partners of teachers know all too well—exhausted, relieved, a hint of exasperation, and clouded by the deep mental fog of processing a hundred tiny, chaos-filled moments.

Ferris doesn't hesitate. He pushes up from his desk, crosses the room, and wraps his arms around her waist, pressing a soft kiss to her lips.

Sloan sighs into the warmth of his embrace, her hands tracing the sharp line of his jaw. "Well," she murmurs, a playful glint in her tired eyes, "I'm much better now."

"Good." Ferris pulls her in closer. "I've got chili finishing up in the crock pot, so we'll be able to eat soon. Just need to wrap up a couple more things for work, and then I'm all yours."

Sloan smiles, stealing another quick kiss before slipping out and gently closing the door behind her, letting him finish up.

Some time passes, and Ferris finally closes his laptop for good. He leans back in his chair, exhaling deeply before adjusting the engagement photo of him and Sloan on his desk. A small smile tugs at his lips.

Satisfied, he pushes up from his chair and heads into the living room. Sloan is curled up on the couch in sweats, her laptop balanced on her legs, a glass of wine within arm's reach. She's always been the type to shed her work clothes the second she gets home, trading structure for comfort without a second thought.

"There's my little wedding planner," Ferris laughs, "what's on the agenda tonight?"

Sloan laughs, "Well right now I'm just working on the wedding day timeline, but enough about that," she closes her laptop. "Let's eat, I'm starving."

Ferris grabs a couple of bowls and pours chili into each one while Sloan gets the table set. They finally sit down to eat. Sloan breathes in the smell of chili and follows it with an audible 'mmm'. As Ferris puts his first spoonful into his mouth, Sloan decides to ask, "Have you talked to Callum at all this week?"

Ferris takes a minute to respond and after he swallows his food, "Come to think of it, no. Why do you ask?"

"Well, we finally got the RSVP card back from him today, but his girlfriend wrote her daughter's name on it," she pauses to see if Ferris heard anything about it, but he looks just as confused. "I just thought it was odd, considering we addressed the envelope to Callum with a plus one."

He reaches a hand to the back of his head, rubbing it absentmindedly, the gesture almost like a reflex, as if the question had added a weight he needed to ease, even if just for a moment. "What do you mean she wrote her daughter's name on it? Like she's trying to say they're bringing her to the wedding?"

Sloan stirs the chili and takes a bite before continuing, "Yeah, she checked yes that they were coming, and at the bottom, she wrote 'and Christy' with a smiley face."

Ferris stiffens. Honestly, in any other situation, it probably wouldn't have been a big deal, but Callum had a history of getting involved with toxic women—ones who were all wrong for him. They saw his weakness, his need to please, and they always knew how to drain him dry.

Ferris could see it now: Gretchen was taking control, and Callum was too passive to stop her. It was bad enough that he was bringing Gretchen to the wedding after how rude and unwelcoming she'd been at the engagement party. But now, they wanted to bring her daughter—who they let roam wild.

"*What?* That's not happening."

"I know, but what are we supposed to do? I feel like things have already been so weird with them, and Gretchen clearly doesn't like us," Sloan takes a sip of her wine. "I don't even get what we did."

Ferris slices some butter to put on a new roll, "Well, I think it's because she wants to control Callum and we can see through her bullshit."

Sloan is growing more irritated by the moment, "I just can't believe she wrote in her daughter's name, like we owe her something after meeting her once and being less than welcoming."

Ferris takes his hand and moves it over to Sloan's, "I know. Look, I didn't want to say anything, but when I talked to Callum last week, he said they already moved in together," Ferris looks away as if it's his bad news he was keeping from Sloan.

Sloan shakes her head, "Wow! Haven't they only been dating a few months? That's fast, even for Callum."

Ferris is holding his lips closed like he's holding a big secret. Sloan looks at him and tilts her head as if to say, *What else?*

He continues, "It's worse, he's paying all the bills."

Sloan's jaw drops. They've been down this road before with Callum. "What? He can barely afford rent for himself. How does he always get caught in these circles?" She notices Ferris is looking uncomfortable in his chair. "Okay, spill, I can tell you've got more to say."

Ferris bites his lip. "I've been sending him money to help him pay bills again."

Sloan doesn't say anything, but a look of disappointment washes over her face. Ferris, knowing this would bother her, continues,

"Look, I know what you're gonna say, and I'm sorry, but he was begging for help, and I said this is the last time, he needs to be better at saving money, and he needs her to chip in more."

Sloan takes both of their plates and walks them over to the sink. "Oh my gosh, I cannot believe he asked you for more money, knowing we're saving up and paying for our own wedding." She places both hands on the counter and takes a deep breath.

Ferris can hear the panic in Sloan's voice and gets up to join her in the kitchen. He stands to the side and puts his hand around her back, "Look, I know. I'm starting to learn my lesson. He was just short a little bit on rent this month, so I said I could give him some money, but that was it."

Sloan is trying to understand—she really is—but it gets harder by the day. "Fine. I want to help your friend, and I'm all for that. But I feel like he's just taking advantage of you."

She pauses, crossing the room to grab the RSVP card, and lets out a slow exhale as she sets it down. "We're done," she says simply.

Ferris frowns. "What do you mean?"

She turns to him, steady now. "No more money. No more favors. No more bending over backward just because Callum can't stand up for himself." She gestures toward the RSVP. "If he can't even respect the terms of a wedding invitation, what makes you think he's going to respect anything else?"

Ferris hesitates, rubbing a hand down his face.

Sloan's voice softens, though her stance doesn't budge. "This is where we stop trying to save him."

There is a beat of silence between them, heavy and unresolved. "Callum's just doing whatever she wants," she adds quietly. "Not thinking for himself... not even trying to take care of himself first. Is he losing his mind?"

Ferris turns Sloan so they're facing each other and puts his hands on her face. "No, I think he just wants someone to love him so bad. He's willing to do anything for that person, which is great, but he's often blinded by what love really is."

Sloan's eyes well up with tears, and she's not sure if it's the stress of wedding planning, or feeling bad for Callum, but either way, it's a release that needs to happen.

Ferris moves his hands down his arms and to her hands. "Don't worry. I'll call Callum tomorrow and handle it."

Chapter 14

The next day, Ferris sits at the kitchen table while Sloan is at work. He absentmindedly flips his phone between his fingers. The RSVP card sits beside him, the words *"and Christy"* practically taunting him. He exhales sharply, rubbing a hand down his face before unlocking his phone and opening the text conversation with Callum.

He wants to call him right then and there, to demand what the hell he's thinking. But he knows he needs to approach it differently. Callum is easily manipulated by the people around him, so he wants to come in as a friend first and see what Callum will reveal.

Ferris sets his phone down and leans back in his chair, staring at the ceiling. He'd been sending Callum money for months now, believing it was helping him get back on his feet. Helping his *best friend* keep a roof over his head. But the last time they talked, Callum had revealed that Gretchen and Christy moved in with him and he was paying for everything. Of course, he shared this tiny detail *after* Ferris sent him the money, so he felt a little off-put. He wanted to tell Sloan right away, but he knew how stressed she was with everything going on with his family and planning the wedding. He didn't want to add another thing into the mix. Thinking about it now, Ferris scoffs, running a hand to the back of his head in frustration.

Finally, he picks up the phone again and clicks on Callum's name. Ferris almost instantly stands and starts walking around to help ease the tension. Within a couple of seconds, Callum picks up and greets Ferris, loudly. "Hey man, long time no talk. How are you guys doing?"

They catch up for a few minutes and Ferris updates him on the wedding progress, Sloan's job, and random small talk reserved for two old neighbors, not two best friends who grew up together. Finally, there's a pause, and Ferris realizes it's his chance to ask him about everything going on with Gretchen and rent.

"Look, Callum, so the reason I'm calling is I wanted to see if you've talked to Gretchen about chipping in more for rent and stuff?" he stops himself from continuing, knowing if he doesn't control himself, he might say something he regrets.

There's a pause and then an audible breath before Callum responds with, "Uh yeah, I brought it up to her."

"Oh! Great, so she's going to start paying her portion, then?" Ferris instantly feels some relief.

But then he hears some hesitation when Callum says, "Yeah, once she gets some things in order, I think she will."

And just like that, the relief is gone. He knows Callum. He probably brought it up quietly to her with his tail between his legs. She got mad and brushed him off. "Does she know you're getting help from me?" Of course, she doesn't. He would never let her in on that for fear she would leave him.

"No, no she doesn't," Callum says quietly but confidently.

"Okay. Well, Cal, you've got to be honest with her about what you can afford because you can't keep living like this. And like I said the last time we talked, I'm done sending you money. Sloan and I have been saving for this wedding, and now that Sloan knows I'm helping you, she's stressed. It's just too much."

Callum has sadness in his voice, "I'm sorry, Fer. And honestly, I'm pretty embarrassed Sloan knows now. I don't want to cause any more stress, I know you have a lot going on," he takes a quick breath and continues. "I've actually been thinking about the wedding and how I can budget for it. How much is the suit rental gonna cost?"

Ferris quickly tries to ease his mind, "Don't worry about that. Anything you need for the wedding I will buy. I want you a part of my wedding because you're a brother to me. I don't care about you buying stuff for it."

"Wow! I really appreciate it, man. You know you and Sloan mean so much to me and I can't imagine not being there for you on your day." There's another brief pause as Ferris works to gather his thoughts on how to bring up the RSVP card situation when Callum continues again. "So, do you think I could have like a hundred and fifty bucks for Gretchen and Christy's dresses?"

Ferris is stunned. Is Callum serious right now? They just talked about this and now, he wants more money. He's not even trying to hide the fact that he's paying for Gretchen anymore, he's just straight-up asking. Ferris feels the words forming before he can stop them. "Yeah, man, I can—"

He catches himself.

Not again. Not this time.

He exhales, forcing himself to see the situation for what it was.

Callum wasn't just in over his head. He wasn't even trying.

Ferris has always thought of Callum as someone who needed help. But maybe that wasn't true.

Maybe he was just someone who took.

Ferris's grip tightens around his phone. "No, of course not," Ferris takes a deep breath. "You've been dating for three months, we hardly know her or her daughter. Why would you be buying dresses for them, let alone me?"

"I don't know, I thought when you said you'd help with anything for the wedding that meant my guest's dresses too. Gretchen started looking at some dresses for her and Christy a couple weeks ago and said she would need my credit card to buy them. I guess I'm getting a little taken advantage of."

After walking around the house through their conversation, Ferris finds himself in his office which seems like a great place to encourage him for this next part, "Yeah, you are *absolutely* being taken advantage of, and while we're on the subject, I did want to let you know that Christy is not invited to the wedding. That's why we only had your name and plus guest on your envelope." Ferris takes a sip of coffee from the mug on his desk. Mid sip he realizes it's cold and from yesterday.

"What? Come on, you guys can just squeeze her in? I mean she doesn't take up much space!" Callum's voice is getting anxious, stressed really. He starts bargaining with Ferris sharing different reasons why Christy should be able to come, how Gretchen will be sitting with her, how Christy is always on her best behavior, but Ferris doesn't budge, and he doesn't hold back.

"I'm sorry, but no, it's not going to work." Ferris explains how Gretchen hardly watched her at the engagement party, she ran around doing whatever he wanted, and provides a brief reminder to Callum that he's not Christy's father and needs to get his life in order before taking on another huge responsibility. Not to mention the fact that Callum is in the wedding, so he'll be busy all morning and won't have time to take care of Gretchen and Christy during it.

Ferris is now feeling that same anxiety he gets when talking to his mom. That pull where you want to help someone and you care about them, but they're just not getting it. Callum was his best friend, but the relationships he got himself into were often exhausting.

No matter what Ferris said, Callum just isn't getting it, and he starts to sound panicked, "Please, Ferris, you guys gotta let Christy come." Callum starts pacing around his apartment looking out the front window to see if Gretchen is home yet.

At this point, Ferris is now lying on his couch in the living room staring up at the ceiling. He wants to say yes, he wants to give in, but he can only imagine how Christy will be on the day of the wedding. So far all scenarios he's thinking about aren't good. "I'm sorry. No, we can't have her come."

There's a long empty silence and then finally a long exhale, "Man, I don't know what I'm gonna tell Gretchen. I hope she comes still," he pauses again before hesitantly saying, "I mean I hope she still wants to be with me."

Ferris begins to explain to Callum that if Gretchen breaks up with him over this she isn't right for him to begin with.

All Callum manages to say is, "Yeah, but you don't know her like I do," before rushing off the phone—Gretchen just got home.

Ferris stares at the screen in disbelief. "Unbelievable." He tosses the phone onto the coffee table and rubs his temples, eyes locked on the display like it might light up again.

It doesn't.

The last time Cal had gone dark like this, Ferris had reached out. He'd texted. Checked in. Asked if he was okay.

He isn't going to do that this time. His fingers twitched to dial back—muscle memory, habit—but he forces them still.

If Cal wants to talk, he'd have to be the one to reach out first.

Chapter 15

A cross town, Callum drops his phone onto the counter, heart pounding. He quickly jumps up to start straightening up when Gretchen walks in with Christy beside her.

Callum turns and forces an exhausted smile, making his way over to her. He gives Christy a high-five and then leans in to give Gretchen a kiss. She pulls back and puts her hand in between their mouths. "No, thanks."

"What's wrong?" Callum looks around, confused.

Gretchen motions for Christy to go play with her toys before striding into the kitchen. She tosses her keys and purse onto the table, then plops into a chair, kicking off her shoes with a huff. "Well, I was paying for gas, and your card declined… again! Do you know how embarrassing that is?"

Callum lets out a nervous laugh. "Oh, that card sure is finicky." His face grows hot, his heart hammering in his chest. He already knows the truth—there is nothing left on that card. He'd maxed it out months ago, stretching every last dollar to keep up with the bills. He wants be a good boyfriend, to make this work, but he isn't sure how much longer he can keep this up. He's barely scraping by.

Gretchen, clearly irritated, scoffs. "Whatever." She snatches up her shopping bags and disappears into their bedroom. She'd been out buying dresses for herself and Christy to wear to the wedding—along with new purses, shoes, and accessories to match.

Callum sits there for a minute wondering if he should follow her into the bedroom, but realizes she probably wants some space. He walks over to sit by Christy, who's now opening up her coloring book. He starts to color with her and make small talk about her day but keeps it pretty light. She looks up at him and asks for an applesauce, so he gets up and walks to the kitchen.

As he rummages through the fridge, a sharp, irritated scoff echoes from the bedroom, followed by the unmistakable slap of a phone hitting the nightstand. Callum freezes, his hand gripping the applesauce pouch a little tighter.

"Are you kidding me?" Gretchen's voice rings out, dripping with frustration.

His stomach tightens. Christy barely glances up from her coloring, clearly used to the outbursts. Callum exhales and hurries toward the bedroom. "What's wrong?"

"I'll be returning these freaking dresses because we're not going to the wedding," Gretchen snaps, yanking them from the closet and shoving them back into the bag beside her.

Callum stands in the doorway, applesauce still in hand, eyes darting between the closet and Gretchen. What could have possibly happened in the past thirty seconds that made her change her mind, "What? What do you mean you're not going? What changed so fast?"

"Oh, not just me and Christy. *You're* not going either," Gretchen says, jabbing a finger at him like she's casting a spell. She starts panic-cleaning the room, her movements sharp and deliberate.

Callum just stands there, eyes darting around like he might find an answer hidden somewhere. "Look, I'm sorry about the card declining, but I swear that was just a fluke. We can afford the dresses, no problem. In fact, Ferris just told me he's paying for my suit, so at least we don't have to worry about that—" The words spill out in a rush, desperate, as if sheer speed can fix this. He's panicking. He'll say anything to make sure she doesn't leave him.

Gretchen freezes mid-motion and scoffs. "What the hell are you talking about? Of course, we can afford the dresses—I already bought them. I'm talking about the incredibly rude message Sloan just sent me." She storms over to the window, arms folded tight as she stares outside.

"Sloan texted you?" Callum's voice is wary, and now he's talking to the back of Gretchen's head.

"Yup. She wanted to 'reaffirm' that Christy's not allowed at their wedding." She pauses, letting the words hang, waiting for a reaction. Nothing. That only fuels her anger. "I mean, what kind of people are you even friends with?" Finally, she turns, eyes locked on him like he personally betrayed her, like this entire mess is his fault.

Callum looks down at the floor and then back over at Gretchen. "That's odd. I can't see Sloan being rude about that," He sits down at the end of the bed. "I meant to talk to you about it. I guess it's a wedding for those 18 and older only."

"Oh, so you're a part of it too? You don't even want Christy to come?" Her words are sharp with accusations.

"No, no, no, that's not what I'm saying," Callum, starting to panic, puts his hand on the back of his neck. "Of course, I want Christy to come. I just got off the phone with Ferris and he just explained to me the whole situation. So, I'm just telling you what I know. I'm not a part of it." He throws his hands up.

Gretchen starts angrily rifling through her things and heads into the living room where Christy is now coloring on the coffee table. Callum follows behind her, unsure of what to say next. Gretchen glances down at Christy, scoffs, and continues to walk by her to the kitchen table. Callum finds a pad of paper, puts it on the table, and motions for Christy to start coloring there. He then continues to follow Gretchen.

She quickly turns to face him. "I don't want to see them, let alone celebrate with them at their wedding. You can call Ferris now and tell him we're not coming."

Chapter 16

Jenny finds herself at her kitchen table, finishing up her Psychology capstone project on attachment styles. It feels like she's been living on coffee for the last month. With everything she's juggling for the wedding, work, and school, she hardly has any downtime for herself. Maybe it was a blessing that Charlie ghosted her, she thinks. There's no way she would even have time for a boyfriend right now—too much of a distraction. She picks up her coffee to take a big gulp when there's a sudden pound on the door.

Her heart immediately starts pounding in sync—she isn't expecting anyone. A small, hopelessly romantic part of her secretly hopes it's Charlie, showing up to sweep her off her feet and apologize for being an idiot. But alas, when she opens the door, it's not Charlie. It's her mother, standing there with a tray of cookies, and a giant bag on her arm, wearing a big smile.

Jenny musters a small smile as her mom breezes past her, making herself at home without so much as an invitation. "Hi Mom, come on in," she whispers to herself as she closes the door behind her. "What brings you over?"

Kate gets an excited look on her face and plops the giant bag on Jenny's kitchen table. "Well, I know things have been a little hectic and weird lately. But I've been thinking about Sloan's bachelorette party. So, what do you think about..." she opens up the bag and puts on blue and white striped sunglasses, a white sash, and a sunhat, "The last sail before the veil," she laughs and hands Jenny an extra sash.

Jenny looks down at it like Kate just handed her a dead snake. "I'm confused, what is all this?"

"It's me, making things right. I'm going to plan and host the bachelorette party!" Kate smiles proudly.

Jenny's eyes dart away and right back at the sash in her hands as she sits down at the kitchen table. "Look, Mom, this is nice, really it is. But this isn't the way to make things right. And I'm sorry, but you're not invited to the bachelorette party."

"What do you mean I'm not invited to the bachelorette party?" Kate rips the hat off her head and sets it on the table. "First the bridal shower, and now this?"

"Mom, the mother of the groom is hardly ever invited to the bachelorette party, so I wouldn't take it personally. Although, maybe after everything, you should." Jenny closes her laptop and grabs her coffee mug off the table.

Kate picks up the hat again, fidgeting with it in her hands. "Well, where are you guys going? I mean, I could pay for the hotel, help save some costs."

Jenny pauses, debating her options. The truth is, she and the other bridesmaids had been planning the bachelorette party for months—everything was booked, paid for, and set in stone. She doesn't need her mom's help, not even a little, and there is no way she's going to let her interfere.

"We're going to Siesta Key, so you probably wouldn't want to go anyway," Jenny smirks as she grabs water from the refrigerator in the kitchen.

Kate's eyes open wide. She walks over to Jenny in the kitchen and plops the hat back on her head, "What do you mean? I love Siesta Key!"

"Well, I'll talk to Sloan, but I can't guarantee anything."

"How about this? Since you're the maid of honor, you send me the link to the hotel, and I'll just buy it for you guys and then you can tell her it was a little gift from me. Maybe then she'll be more inclined."

"That's very kind of you, but it's already all been paid for. Every single girl that's going is splitting the cost."

"Just send me what the cost was, and I will send you the money for it," she isn't giving up. So, Jenny just tells her she'll send her the cost and allow her to pay for it. "Great. Now, what are the dates so I can block it off my calendar?"

Jenny thinks fast, willing to test her boundaries. "It's next weekend. But again, that's not a guarantee that you can come."

"Oh, next weekend? That's so soon." She pulls out her phone and starts to add some notes to her calendar. She then stops to look up and notices Jenny's face is unamused. "Um, okay, yeah—no, of course. I totally understand." Jenny tells her mom she needs to focus on her paper tonight. Her mom gets the hint and heads toward the door, but before she leaves, she turns and gestures to the bag she left on the table. "Keep it," she says. "For planning inspiration."

Jenny forcefully smiles and closes the door behind her mother.
***

It's been a few days and Ferris still hasn't heard back from Callum. The last time they talked, Callum said he would talk to Gretchen about the wedding and have her help pay some of the bills. However, Ferris was hardly convinced. Later that night when Sloan got home from work, he caught her up on everything that happened. After telling her that Callum had sheer panic in his voice at the thought of Gretchen possibly breaking up with him, they realized there was probably a slim chance that he would actually tell Gretchen that Christy couldn't come to the wedding.

They decided together that Sloan would reach out to Gretchen and send a friendly text about the wedding:

Hey Gretchen! We're so excited that you and Callum will be celebrating with us on our big day, we can't wait to see you both! Just a quick note—our wedding is an adults-only event, so we wanted to clarify that the invite was just for the two of you. We totally understand how tricky childcare can be, and we hope you're still able to join us for the celebra-

tion! Let us know if you have any questions. Can't wait to celebrate with you!"

"Still no reply from Gretchen, either?" Ferris walks into the kitchen where Sloan is making coffee.

She shakes her head and rereads the text, double-checking that it didn't come across as rude. Maybe she had the wrong number, though that seemed unlikely.

"At this point, I'm thinking it would be a blessing if Gretchen broke up with him, but who knows where that would lead him," Ferris mutters, anxiously scrolling on his phone. "I'm just really disappointed he's acting like we don't matter to him anymore."

A sudden knock at the door makes Sloan turn mid-pour, nearly spilling her coffee. "Oh, that's Jenny! She's coming over to finalize bachelorette party details." She excitedly sets down the carafe and scoots past Ferris to answer the door.

Jenny stands there, her hair pulled up into a messy bun, and sunglasses perched on her head. She's dressed in an oversized maroon sweatshirt and black leggings, looking both casual and ready to get things done. "Maid of honor here, reporting for duty!" She playfully salutes, standing up straighter with a smirk. "Alright, Sloan, you got everything ready for our trip tomorrow?" She pulls her into a hug before striding into the kitchen, where Ferris is still standing.

Ferris gives her a quick hug before taking another bite of his breakfast sandwich.

Sloan follows behind, grinning from ear to ear. "Yes! I finished packing last night—well, mostly. I'm sure I'll still throw a few things in today."

Ferris chuckles. "You call the disaster that hit our room 'done packing'?"

Sloan rolls her eyes. "Okay, maybe it's not actually packed, but everything is laid out by day, so I know *what* will be packed."

Jenny holds up a finger to his mouth. "Shhh! You're the groom. You have *no* say in the matter. We're about to have the trip of a lifetime—warm weather, no men, no responsibilities." She throws her hands up dramatically as if basking in imaginary sun rays.

Ferris raises a brow. "Is this *your* vacation or Sloan's?"

Jenny snaps out of it, shooting him a playful glare. "It's *all* of ours! We're here to celebrate this fabulous woman." She turns to Sloan with a grin. "Speaking of which, check your email. A little pre-bachelorette gift from me."

Sloan pulls out her phone and starts clicking around. "Okay, let's see... wait." Her eyes widened. "You bumped me up to *first class*?" She lets out a squeal and rushes over to hug Jenny. "Oh my gosh, you're the *best* maid of honor ever!"

Jenny hesitates, her expression dimming just slightly. "Yeah, well... you can thank my mom for that."

Sloan and Ferris exchange a look, but before either can ask, Jenny grabs her coffee and changes the subject. "Anyway! We leave tomorrow, and I don't want any wedding talk. Just sun, drinks, and relaxation."

Chapter 17

Later that evening, Kate pulls up a travel site on her laptop, her lips pressed into a firm line. "All right, let's see flights to Sarasota." She's sitting on the couch in front of the TV, legs propped up on the coffee table.

Ted overhears her from the other room and shuffles over to her, realizing she's probably doing something she shouldn't be, "Kate, what are you doing?"

Kate jumps in her seat. "Oh gosh, Ted, you scared me. What do you mean what am I doing? I'm just relaxing on my laptop. She looks up at him and smiles.

Ted rolls his eyes and takes a deep breath. "Kate, I'm not dumb, I know what you're doing. Have you not learned from last time? You can't just book a flight and show up when you're not invited."

Kate does what she does best and scoffs, "Ted, I paid for the hotel, and it was *not* cheap. So, let me just tell you, they're kind of obligated to invite me." She continues to click around on her computer while he stands there overlooking her.

"No, I don't think that's how it works, Kate. You're just gonna make this worse for everybody," Ted crosses his arms.

Kate doesn't look up from her laptop as she continues to speak. "Here's the problem. Sloan hasn't yet met the fun-vacation-Kate. Once I get there and I'm sipping a margarita on the beach, it's going to be a new me!" She sets her laptop down, dramatically mimicking sipping a margarita. "It'll all be fine. You're freaking out over nothing."

Ted just looks at her, blinks a couple of times, and walks away, shaking his head.

Kate plops back down on the couch, picking her laptop back up. "And done!" She clicks the final button to purchase the flight. "Bachelorette party, here we come!"

***

It's the day of the bachelorette party and Jenny pulls up in a stretch limo to surprise Sloan, sending her a quick text to let her know she's arrived.

Sloan receives the text as she's walking out of her bedroom, rolling her luggage behind her with sunglasses on her head. Her long hair holds loose curls and she's wearing bright red lipstick. She walks towards the office door where Ferris is propped up getting some work done.

"Jenny just texted me, so I'm heading out!"

Ferris jumps up from his desk and wraps his arms around her. "All right, you have the best time ever, babe. And don't forget to call me when you land." He places a gentle kiss on her forehead, grabbing her luggage from her, and leading her out the garage.

"Who do you think I am? I'm going to text you when we're almost at the airport, text you when we get to the airport, text you when I get to the gate, and text you when we take off. And then I'll call you when we land," Sloan laughs as she brushes her hair to one side of her shoulder.

Ferris opens the door to the garage and presses the button to open it. "Alright, whatever helps you feel better, but once you get there, don't even think of me, just have fun with your girls."

As the garage finishes opening, they see Jenny standing in front of the limo, arms outstretched, sunglasses on, in a long black dress.

Sloan's eyes open wide and her jaw drops. "Oh my gosh, a limo?!" She runs up to Jenny and practically pushes her over.

Ferris hands the driver Sloan's luggage. "You really outdid yourself, Jenny!" Ferris says while smiling, then turns back to Sloan. "Alright, you go get out of here and have an amazing time! Let your worries fade away."

Sloan, still admiring the limo, turns to him, "What worries?" She winks and swoops in for a big kiss before readjusting her purse strap over her body. "Bye honey, I love you!" The driver opens up the car door and Jenny leads the way in as Sloan follows.

Ferris says his "I love you" and heads back inside.

Sloan slams the door and turns to Jenny. "This is crazy! How much money did you spend?"

Jenny laughs as she grabs a bottle of champagne and starts to pour her a glass, "Oh this old thing? You can thank my mom for it."

She hands Sloan a glass that foams over the top. Sloan quickly takes a sip, "Wow. She's really trying to suck up to me, isn't she?" She takes another big sip from her champagne.

Jenny pours herself a glass and motions for them to clink their glasses. "Sure, you could say that. Just wait to thank her until after we get back from the trip." The limo pulls away and they head off to pick up the other bridesmaids on the way to the airport.

The limo finally arrives and they quickly get out of the car to start their vacation. The automatic doors slide open, and a gust of cold, air-conditioned airport air rushes past them as Sloan, Jenny, and the bridesmaids step inside. The terminal buzzes with early-morning travelers, rolling suitcases clicking against the tile, voices blending into an indistinct hum of announcements, chatter, and footsteps echoing through the wide space.

Jenny pushes her sunglasses up onto her head and adjusts her tote bag. "Alright, ladies, vacation has officially started," she announces, striding forward with the confidence of someone who's been waiting her whole life to take charge of a bachelorette trip.

They get their bags checked, get through security, and weave through the terminal, dodging frantic travelers and families corralling overtired kids. Jenny, in full Maid of Honor mode, pulls out her phone and checks the departures board. "Gate C17," she announces, looking around. "Aha! There it is! She points down the way a little bit."

"Oh perfect! And it's right next to a bar, I say we stop there first," Sloan laughs.

"Alright, you heard her ladies, off to the bar!" Jenny flips her hair and leads the way as Sloan and the others follow.

They make their way and see five bar seats open, so they throw their stuff down and take a seat. As the bartender walks over Jenny jumps in before anyone can order, "Hi, we'll take five tequila shots and then whatever they all want to sip on," she starts to shuffle in her bag, "and you can put it all on this. Do not let this girl pay for anything!" She hands the bartender her credit card and gestures towards Sloan.

Just then she feels a vibration in her back pocket.

She lets out a heavy sigh when she sees her mom's name flashing on the screen.

"Um, I gotta take this. I'm just gonna step over by the gate where it's a little quieter. I'll be right back," she tells Sloan and her friends.

Grabbing the shot the bartender just set down, she throws it back in one swift motion, then turns and walks off, phone already pressed to her ear.

Taking another deep breath, she answers her phone, "Hey mom, what's up?" She looks around nervously as she talks, hoping her mom didn't follow her there.

The other end of the phone sounds muffled, "Hey honey, it's me. It's kind of loud where you're at. Where are you?"

Jenny walks over to the gate and finds a seat to sit down, "Oh, I'm at the mall. I had to run an errand really quick." She notices a big family walking over like they are about to sit down next to her. She quickly stands up to walk away and avoid any more sounds.

"Oh, I didn't know you still shopped at the mall. But, okay, listen, you never got back to me about what Sloan said about the bachelorette party. I even texted you yesterday," Kate adds.

"Oh, yeah, I completely forgot. I'm so sorry," she notices Sloan and her friends down the way at the bar, laughing and she finds herself wishing she didn't answer.

"So, can I come?"

It takes a minute for Jenny to realize Kate's asking for a response, "Look, Mom, I just don't think it's a good idea." She needs to get off the phone now, she's missing out.

Jenny starts to tell her mom she has to go when she cuts in. "Alright, well, I have to tell you something. I already bought a ticket so I'm coming," she pauses as if waiting for Jenny to share some excitement.

Jenny's not the least bit shocked, she knew she would do this, knew she couldn't understand no. "Interesting, you know Mom, I had a feeling you would say that."

Kate smiles to herself, proudly. Jenny is finally getting it. She can't leave her mom out of everything anymore. She belongs with them. "Yeah, so look I was wondering if you wanted to drive together or meet at the airport."

Jenny thinks fast. "Oh, so I ended up switching up the date so I'm actually gonna get there a day before you." She finds herself walking through Hudson News looking at all the magazine covers.

Kate doesn't say anything, she just looks through the calendar on her phone wondering why Jenny would make such a last-minute change. "Oh really? That's interesting. Why did you do that?"

"Last-minute deal on flights, plus I wanted to get early and set up," she grabs a water bottle and a pack of gum and sets it on the counter. "So why don't you just meet us at the hotel when you get in? I'll give you the address." Jenny pays and starts to walk back towards the girls.

Kate is now standing in her closet going through outfits to back for her trip, holding them up one by one in front of the mirror. "Well, that would be great thanks for being so understanding and helpful honey. See you in Siesta Key!"

They say their goodbyes and Jenny walks back to join Sloan and her friends at the bar.

As Sloan sees her coming, she grabs a drink and holds her hand out to hand it to her. "Come on! You've got some catching up to do."

Jenny laughs and quickly grabs the drink, "Margarita?"

Sloan smiles, "Yup! What did your mom want?"

"Oh, nothing. She just wanted to make sure we got to the airport okay." Jenny grabs her drink and takes a big sip. They sit together for almost an hour, laughing and planning out the bachelorette party before heading over to the gate.

Right then, the gate attendant makes the announcement, "All right, everyone. Thank you for your patience. We will now be boarding Flight 237 from Milwaukee to Nashville."

Jenny stands up to get in line to board, "All right, that's us."

Sloan gets up to follow, "Nashville, here we come."

***

The next day, Kate finds herself having a fantastic morning. She arrived at the airport early, had plenty of time for a cup of coffee, and read the entire flight. She even landed in Sarasota 30 minutes earlier than expected.

She texts Jenny that she landed but gets no response. She figures she must be busy setting up the hotel room, so she doesn't keep pushing. She hops in a cab and heads off to the hotel where everyone's staying. She tries calling Jenny from the cab, but no response.

When the cab pulls up, she gets out and waits for the driver to get her luggage for her. She grabs the key Jenny left for her at the front desk and heads to the room.

"317... 317, oh—there it is!" She walks up to the door and knocks, calling out, "Knock, knock! Surprise! I'm here!"

No answer.

She knocks harder. "Hello? Girls?! This is ridiculous!" She pulls out the key card and holds it to the reader. When it flashes green, she quickly opens the door. "Jenny? Sloan?"

But the room is empty. No luggage. No coats. No sign anyone had ever been there—just a clean room, perfectly untouched.

She grabs her phone to call Jenny again.

"Hey, Mom, what's up?"

"Jenny, what the heck? I've been trying to get a hold of you all morning! I've been pounding on the hotel door, and now I'm in the hotel room and no one is here. Where the heck are you girls?"

"Well, that's weird because I have the door open, and I don't see you."

Kate looks around, "I'm confused."

"Well, what town are you in?"

"I'm in the Siesta Key. Where the heck else would I be?" Kate is growing impatient, she taps her fingers on the wall beside her.

"Oh, darn it. Silly me," Jenny smacks her forehead, "I forgot to tell you there was a slight change of plans. We're in Nashville! But anyway, I gotta go, our lunch just got here, and we've got a busy day ahead of us. Have fun in Siesta Key, Mom!"

Kate stands there, jaw dropped. "Jennifer Kathleen... you better be joking right now. Jenny? Jenny?"

The line goes dead.

She grips her phone, heart hammering as she looks out her window.

She was in Siesta Key.
They were in Nashville.

Unbelievable.

Her fingers move before she even has time to think.

Jenny's phone now goes straight to voicemail. Ferris's does the same. Sloan's just keeps ringing.

Fine.

She pulls up Facebook.

"Some people just don't understand the meaning of family. It's so sad when you raise a son who turns his back on you."

She hit *Post*. The comments started rolling in immediately.

Perfect.

Part 5

Chapter 18

With Sloan away at her bachelorette party, Ferris finds himself sitting in his home office, head down, reviewing a project timeline to ensure all tasks are on track before the weekend. He feels the warm sun from the window on the back of his neck, taking a deep breath before picking up his coffee.

Sloan wasn't loud by any means but having her away made the house feel too quiet. He likes having her around, but he knows she really needs this weekend to let loose after the stress she has been under.

He's been finding it really difficult to know what to do in this situation with his mom. He *knows* what he should do for Sloan, but it doesn't make it any easier.

He's used to his mom acting this way, way before Sloan, even, so he hates to say it, but he isn't completely shocked. This Callum thing, though, was new. Callum has been his best friend for years now. They always have each other's backs. Sure, he never had the best taste in women, but he never let them get in the way of their friendship before.

Ferris picks up his cell phone and notices a text he missed from Sloan—a picture of her and Jenny at brunch with bloody marys sitting in front of them. The large kind, with practically a whole meal sticking out of it. Sloan's hair is curled and she's wearing a white off-the-shoulder top. Ferris smiles to himself and realizes how much he misses her already.

Just then, a text pops up on the screen from Callum:

Hey man, I hate to do this, but with everything going on, I'm just not going to be able to come to your wedding anymore. Sorry.

Ferris stares at his phone for a few seconds, squinting, as if trying to decipher a foreign language. *Not coming to the wedding?* What the hell does he mean he's not coming? His heart pounds faster, a mix of anger and anxiety rising in his chest. He sits there, dumbfounded, wondering what kind of nonsense Gretchen had spewed to convince Callum that staying home was better than celebrating his best friend's wedding.

For a moment, he debates driving straight to Callum's house. But if he saw Gretchen's face, he wasn't sure he could hold back his frustration. *Enough is enough.* Ferris grabs his phone, stands up from his desk, and starts pacing as he dials Callum's number.

Callum must have been anxiously checking his phone because without missing a beat, he picks up. "Hey Fer, how's it going?"

Ferris feels his face getting hot and takes a deep breath to help speak level-headedly. "How's it going? How's it *going*? Um, pretty shitty considering my best friend of 15 years just *texted* me without explanation to tell me he's not coming to my wedding anymore." Ferris hears a breath on the other line like Callum is about to start talking, but Ferris continues, "What do you mean you're not coming?"

Callum quickly walks into his bedroom to hear better, since Christy is watching TV in the living room. "Hey, Ferris. Yeah, look, uh, it's just not gonna work out."

"You say it's just not gonna work out when you're going to break up with someone, not when you're not gonna show up to your best friend's wedding, you're supposed to be my best man." Ferris is growing more and more impatient, pacing the hall of their home.

Callum is now sitting on the edge of his bed when Gretchen walks into the room and stands at the doorway. She leans against the frame, arms folded, and legs crossed. Her strawberry-blonde hair is pushed behind her ears and she looks less than amused, watching over Callum checking his every word.

Callum nervously looks at her while he responds, "Yeah, well, I don't know what else you want me to say. We just have a lot going on that month and it's just not going to be a good time." He looks down at the floor, realizing he's not making any sense, but he feels helpless.

"Not gonna be a good time? I don't get what you're trying to say. Is Gretchen there? What is *she* making you say?" He finds himself in the kitchen, he pulls out a water bottle from the fridge and starts to chug it. Callum is silent. "You can't just dip out of my wedding for no reason and expect me to not call you up and see what's going on."

Callum stands up off the bed and starts to leave the room to talk to Ferris alone, but Gretchen follows.

"Well, there's not *no* reason," he's still walking around the apartment trying to find a quiet place to talk, but Gretchen is still right behind him. He ends up back in their room. "We can't go because there's no one to watch Christy."

Ferris throws his hand out as if to say 'and there it is!' "Callum, tell me why it's your responsibility that your girlfriend of three months has no one to watch her daughter."

Gretchen looks at Callum and mouths, "Put it on speaker." Callum is visibly flustered. He hesitantly but quickly removes his phone from his ear and turns on the speaker. "Because this isn't just some girl, Ferris. This is a very serious relationship I'm in and if you want us both to be able to come then Christy needs to be able to come too."

Gretchen smiles proudly, as if she fed the lines to him herself.

"Look, it's not Christy's fault, and nothing against her, but I saw how Gretchen neglected her at the engagement party. Christy was running all over, spilling food and drinks on the floor, and Gretchen did nothing to help the situation."

Gretchen's face is turning red, and she starts moving closer to Callum like she's going to say something, but Callum puts up his hand to tell her to wait.

Ferris continues, "Gretchen was less than friendly, and never even made it a point to try to get to know us. Don't you see it? She's using you! At this point, she should be lucky she's even getting an invite."

Gretchen is about to burst at the seams. She puts her tongue to the front of her teeth and squints, yanking the phone out of Callum's hand. He jumps up and tries to get it back, but Gretchen turns and walks away as he now follows behind. "Hi, Ferris. It's Gretchen. I've been listening the whole time, and I think the way you're talking is disgusting. I don't really appreciate all the things that you're saying to Callum about me, thinking I wasn't here, and saying I'm using him."

"Okay, Gretchen, so tell me, what have you done for Callum these last few months?"

Gretchen is speechless and instead starts to go off about how Sloan has been disrespectful to her since the moment they met. Her voice drips with the kind of condescension that makes Ferris's skin crawl. She's throwing around words like "rude" and "unfair," twisting the situation to make Sloan the villain as if the entire wedding revolved around her ability to waltz in and make a scene.

Ferris barely hears her anymore. His mind is too busy running through every red flag, every moment Callum had brushed off as nothing—how he always footed the bill, how Gretchen conveniently always had an excuse, how every disagreement somehow ended with Callum apologizing.

And now she is driving a wedge into a friendship that had lasted longer than any relationship she'd ever been in.

Ferris exhales slowly, steadying his temper. He won't give her the reaction she wants. But one thing is clear—this isn't just about the wedding anymore. Ferris can feel his patience thinning with every word Gretchen spits into the phone. It isn't just the arrogance in her tone—it's the way she speaks with complete certainty as if she had the right to dictate who's welcome at his wedding and who isn't.

He can hear Callum in the background, saying something too quiet to make out, but Gretchen steamrolls right over him. Of course, she does. That was what she did best—control the narrative and twist reality until it suited her.

Ferris lets out a sharp breath, rubbing his temple. "You know what, Gretchen? I think we both know exactly what this is about."

"Enlighten me," she shoots back.

"Control," Ferris says sharply. "You're using Callum, and if he doesn't have his close friends around, you get more of it."

Gretchen lets out a dry laugh. "Using him for what?"

Ferris doesn't hesitate. "Well, let's see," he says, "It was pretty convenient that you started dating him right after you got kicked out of your last apartment. And even more convenient that you moved in with him after only three months of dating. Shall I go on?"

Ferris clenches his jaw as his mind races through all the late-night calls from Callum—the panic in his voice over bills, the quiet shame when he admitted he was short on rent again. He thinks about the times he covered for his friend, no questions asked, the countless Venmo transfers sent first thing in the morning, the groceries bought without a second thought. Callum never had to ask—Ferris just knew. He had grown up with more, and helping his best friend had always felt like the right thing to do.

But now, listening to Gretchen sneer at him through the phone while Callum sat silent, not stepping in, not defending him—it made Ferris's blood boil. His fingers curl tighter around his phone as betrayal settles deep in his chest, hot and suffocating. He exhales sharply, forcing himself to keep it together. He wants to lay it all out, to make her see the truth, but something holds him back.

Then, Gretchen delivers the final blow.

"It's not my fault Callum wants to spend money on me and take care of me. Maybe you should learn from him and treat your girlfriend that way. It's not my fault you're insecure that he treats me like a queen."

Ferris goes still. His grip on the phone turns white-knuckle tight, his pulse roaring in his ears. That was it. Loyalty be damned. His restraint snaps like a brittle wire.

"Number one, Sloan is my fiancée," he shoots back, his voice sharp as a blade. "Number two, if you want to cut me out of your lives, that's fine. But you're going to need to cut back on a *lot* of things."

A beat of silence. Then—

Callum finally speaks, his voice rushed, panicked. "Alright, enough is enough. We gotta go."

He reaches for the phone, but Gretchen twists away, holding it tighter, her sharp gaze locking onto him in warning—*Don't you dare hang up.*

Her voice is slow, calculating. "Why would cutting you out mean we have to cut back on things?"

The question was for Ferris, but her eyes stay locked on Callum.

Ferris doesn't hesitate. "Oh, did Callum forget to mention that I've been helping him pay bills for the last six months?"

The second the words leave his mouth, he feels the weight of them. The truth had been set free, and it was too late to take it back.

Gretchen's expression shifts—first confusion, then realization. She turns to Callum, searching his face, her lips parting as the pieces click into place.

Callum looks like he wants to disappear.

And just like that, the house of lies he'd built came crumbling down. And with that, Ferris says a quick goodbye and hangs up the phone.

Gretchen stands there, arms folded tight across her chest, her nails digging into her skin. Her expression shifts—anger flickering in her eyes, but beneath it, something else. Fear. Disbelief. Betrayal.

"I can't believe you," she mutters, her voice cold and clipped. She doesn't wait for a response. Instead, she reaches past Callum, snatching her purse off the bed with a sharp tug before spinning on her heel. Her movements are quick and frantic, her breath shallow as she storms toward the living room.

Without hesitation, she grabs Christy's arm, her grip firm, almost desperate. Christy barely has time to react before she's being pulled toward the door.

Callum watches in stunned silence, his pulse hammering in his ears as Gretchen marches straight to the kitchen counter. She swipes up her keys and phone in one swift motion, her shoes clicking against the tile.

"Gretch, hold on a second—" Callum moves after her, but she doesn't even glance back.

She makes a beeline for the front door, yanking it open so hard it slams against the wall. Still gripping Christy's wrist, she pulls her through the doorway and into the cool air. Christy stumbles slightly, her bare feet skidding against the pavement.

"Gretchen, wait!" Callum shouts, desperation cracking his voice as he chases after her. "Will you just listen?"

Gretchen whips around, yanking Christy with her. "How dare you embarrass me like that, Callum? You've been lying to me for three months—acting like you're some amazing guy who can take care of me. But you can't."

Callum's pulse is hammering, sweat trickling down his forehead. "I know, but I was afraid if I told you the truth, you wouldn't respect me. You wouldn't want to be with me." His voice wavers, but he pushes through. "You suggested moving in so quickly, then started asking for money, my credit card... I just wanted to help."

Christy struggles against Gretchen's grip until she finally breaks free, stumbling backward and landing in a puddle with a splash. She whimpers, but Gretchen barely spares her a glance. Instead, she rolls her eyes. "Oh, so now you're blaming me because you're a loser?"

Callum had heard plenty from Gretchen in the months they'd been together. But *loser* stings. Maybe because deep down, he's always feared it was true—never enough, always needing saving, never quite worthy. Not of Gretchen. Not even Ferris.

But something shifts.

His jaw tightens as he straightens. "If I'm such a loser, why were you with me in the first place?"

Gretchen smirks, flipping her hair over her shoulder. "Lapse of judgment, I guess."

That's it. Callum shakes his head and strokes his forehead with his fingertips, "Wow, after everything I did for you these last few months? Ferris was right about you. He's always been right about you."

They stand there in the apartment parking lot for a few minutes, going back and forth until Callum tells her to grab all her things because she will never be stepping foot in their apartment again.

Gretchen scoffs, arms crossed. "Excuse me? You're not gonna tell me what to do."

Callum exhales sharply, tired of the back and forth. "I think I just did. This is my place. I pay the bills. Grab your stuff and leave. For good."

Gretchen's expression flickers with panic before she masks it with indifference. "I'll be out by next week, okay?"

Callum shakes his head. "No, I'm not waiting until next week. You're out tonight."

Her mouth parts slightly. "What? But, Callum, I have nowhere to go tonight."

His patience is gone. "You have plenty of places. Your parents live twenty minutes away—go there."

Gretchen shifts on her feet, her confidence slipping. "No, please, come on. Just let me stay the night."

Callum laughs, but there's no humor in it. "Funny. You had no problem calling me a loser when you thought you had control. But the second I take my power back, you start begging me for help." He tilts his head. "Who's the loser now?"

Gretchen's lips press into a thin line. She doesn't say anything, but she looks at Christy and then back at Callum.

Callum sighs, glancing at Christy, who is still standing awkwardly nearby. His voice softens just a fraction. "If it weren't for Christy, I'd be kicking you out right now. But because she's here, you get one more night. That's it." He steps back, pulling his keys out of his pocket. "I'm leaving. Pack up your stuff. I don't want to see you when I'm back tomorrow morning."

Chapter 19

Sloan finds herself laughing more than she has in weeks. Her bachelorette weekend has been exactly what she needed—a whirlwind of music, cocktails, and the kind of belly laughs that left her cheeks sore. Surrounded by her closest friends, she feels light, untethered, as if, for just one weekend, the weight of everything happening back home doesn't exist.

As she slips off her boots and lays back in her hotel room bed for the last night, she lets out a satisfied sigh. "I really needed this," she turns to Jenny, packing up her things for their morning flight.

"Oh, I know you did," Jenny replies with a proud little smile, feeling like she's finally brought some calm into a chaotic time.

The next morning, they get into the Uber and head to the airport. The neon lights of the city blur into the distance as reality starts to settle back in—the wedding planning, the tension with Gretchen, the drama with Kate.

For now, though, she holds onto her time away just a little longer, savoring the peace before the storm. The truth is, while she loves her life with Ferris and is mostly excited for the future ahead, she has a lot of fear. She wonders if these are all signs from the universe to run. Their relationship is great and he takes care of her, but was it worth all the baggage that came along with it?

Sloan gets along with almost everyone, but she can't stand Kate—the way she degraded her, spoke condescendingly, and ignored every boundary they had ever tried to set. Just the thought of seeing Kate makes her skin crawl, and she isn't sure she can live with it. Ferris constantly reassures her that he is on her side, which she appreciates, but she can't bear the pressure of feeling like he has to choose between them.

A few hours later, the girls land and catch an Uber home. Between bouts of drifting in and out of sleep, Sloan barely registers the ride until the car finally pulls up to her and Ferris's house. She turns to Jenny with a tired smile, thanking her one last time before grabbing her bags and stepping out of the car.

She walks through the front door, expecting silence, but instead, Ferris is already there, waiting with a coffee in hand. A slow smile spreads across his face.

"Welcome home," he says, opening his arms for her. "How was the flight?"

He's wearing a black hoodie, a backward black ball cap, and *those* grey sweatpants—the ones that should be considered a public service. A grin tugs at her lips. Maybe she was exhausted a minute ago, but suddenly, she's wide awake.

She falls into Ferris's embrace and takes a deep inhale. He always smells so good. "It's so good to be home. I missed you," she pulls back to respond. "The flight was great. I slept pretty much the whole way. The weekend was just amazing. Per usual, Jenny went above and beyond. I'll tell you about it later, for now, I just want this."

She melts into Ferris's embrace, breathing him in like a comfort she didn't realize she had been missing so much. His hands find hers, warm and steady, as he leads her toward the couch.

"You must be exhausted," he murmurs, brushing a strand of hair from her face.

"A little," she admits, tilting her chin up toward him, "but I'd rather spend time with you first."

Ferris gives her that look—the one that makes her heart stutter, the one that tells her he missed her just as much. He pulls her in, his lips lingering just long enough to make her stomach tighten.

Before she can say another word, he's lifting her effortlessly into his lap, a playful grin on his lips. "Then let's make up for lost time."

Laughter mixes with quiet sighs as fingers trace familiar paths, hands exploring in the way only two people who know each other by heart can. The rest of the world fades away, the weight of the weekend slipping from her shoulders as she sinks into him.

Hours later, as the golden hues of sunset filtered through the windows, the laughter quieted, replaced by the kind of comfortable stillness that only comes with knowing someone deeply. But as Ferris sits beside her, his fingers idly tracing circles on her knee,

Sloan can sense the shift—something heavier lingering between them, unspoken but impossible to ignore.

"Alright, I can tell something's off. What's on your mind?"

Ferris takes a breath and readjusts himself on the couch so he's now sitting forward. Sloan places her hand on his back. "So, I had a chat with Callum and Gretchen yesterday. He's stepping down... well not coming at all to the wedding, now."

Sloan bolts upright, "What? He's not going to be a part of it at all now?"

Ferris pulls his hat off his head and flips it around in his hands. "I guess not. He's blinded by her and couldn't give a shit about a 15-year friendship, it seems." He puts his hat back on his head.

Sloan leans back on the couch, eyes wide, wondering why all these issues with everyone suddenly seemed to surface the moment they got engaged. At this point, she's just waiting for the next problem to drop.

As if reading her mind, Ferris sighs. "I don't get it. Why is all this drama coming from every direction now? Was it always there, and we just didn't see it?"

Sloan shifts, tucking her legs under her. "Well... I actually think things are turning a new leaf with your mom—at least a little." She tells him about how Kate upgraded her seat to first class, surprised her with the limo, and paid for the hotel. It didn't erase the past, but for once, Kate actually respected boundaries and just helped without forcing her way in.

Ferris stands, stretching. "You know what? I'll take that as good news. In fact, I think that calls for some wine." He heads to the kitchen and pours two glasses.

Sloan laughs, shaking her head. "Thanks, but I'm on an alcohol sabbatical until the wedding. Jenny kept me well hydrated."

"Suit yourself," Ferris says, pouring her share into his own glass. Just as he lifts it to take a sip, his phone buzzes in his pocket. He glances down and raises an eyebrow. "Well, speak of the devil. My mom's calling—give me a sec."

He answers in the kitchen, his voice bright. "Hey, Mom!"

Sloan stays on the couch, listening to the warmth in his tone, and suddenly wonders—was it a mistake to tell him about Kate's kindness? Would he take it as a full pardon?

Then Kate's voice cuts through the speaker, sharp and unwavering. "I've tried to be nice, Ferris. I've tried everything to turn this whole thing around. But she has now taken it too far, and I'm done."

Chapter 20

Sloan starts to stand, but before she can move closer, Ferris is already rounding the corner toward their bedroom. She hesitates, then slowly creeps through the kitchen, stopping at the edge of the hallway. Peering out, she strains to listen.

From the other room, Ferris tries to calm down Kate, "Mom, what are you talking about?"

Kate's tongue clicks sharply. "I'm done trying with her," she spits, dragging out *her* like saying Sloan's name might burn a hole through her tongue. "I tried apologizing, I tried making things right. I even helped with the bachelorette party. And what does she do? She throws it all back in my face—just to embarrass me."

Scenarios keep running through his head of what Sloan could have possibly done to embarrass his mom. Sloan was just saying she was starting to feel positive about everything. Was she telling the truth? No...no. Of course, she was telling the truth. Right? "I'm still not understanding. What did she do that was so awful?" His fingers press firmly on the back of his neck.

Kate's voice rises, shrill and unsteady, teetering between desperation and fury. She clings to her version of the truth like a lifeline, twisting every detail to paint herself as the victim. Her breath comes faster, her words tumbling out in frantic waves, as if the harder she insists, the more real it will become. "You're telling me you have no idea what she did? Why don't you go ask her then? She can't lie in front of me."

Sloan starts to back away from the closed bedroom door. As much as she wants to listen in, she does not want to be pulled into this conversation to defend herself against the insanity Kate is bringing upon them.

"Look, I would but she's not home right now," Ferris lies, hoping it helps protect Sloan. Although he's realizing at this point there's no winning, he has to make a clear choice.

Kate's speaking faster, "Oh, must be really nice. Guess where I am right now?"

Ferris quietly mutters that she's probably home with Dad.

"No, I'm in Siesta Key. I thought I was here for Sloan's bachelorette party, but to my surprise, no one was here." She decides to take this as an opportunity to rip into everything she hates about Sloan. "Ferris, don't you see it? Sloan is a lying, vindictive woman, and if she would lie to me about something like a bachelorette party, she'd lie to you about anything. Can't you see I'm protecting you?"

Ferris stands silent for a beat, his hand gripping the edge of the counter as his mind races. He takes a deep breath, running a hand through his hair. "I don't know, Mom. I need a minute. I'm still really confused about this whole situation. I don't think Sloan lied to you."

Kate scoffs, her tone sharp as she paces the room, each step filled with indignation. "Call it what you want Ferris, but she never even gave a definite answer or sent me a proper invite to the party. So here I am, stranded all by myself. Why would she do this to me?"

Ferris narrows his eyes, trying to process the words. "So, it's her fault because she didn't invite you to the bachelorette party? Her own mom wasn't even invited." His voice is calm but strained as if trying to keep the conversation from spiraling. "It sounds like Jenny was behind the planning."

"You're not understanding! I paid for everything! Where did my money even go then? She's probably off using it to pay for the wedding. We all know teachers don't make much." Her voice is condescending, talking about Sloan like she's a piece of gum on the bottom of her shoe.

Ferris rolls his eyes and crosses his arms, leaning back in his chair. "Okay, well, again—I'm only getting part of the story, so I'm just putting the pieces together." His voice softens slightly as he tries to make sense of it all. "From what you've said, it sounds like you weren't invited to the bachelorette party. And honestly, with everything that's gone on these past few months, I don't know what would possess you to think she'd even want you there." We're at the point of no return now.

In the hotel bathroom, Kate stands in front of the mirror, fixing her hair. "Whatever, this is ridiculous. I should've known you wouldn't have my back in this," she snaps, frustration rising. "You can't even see it—you're just blinded by her. Ever since she came into your life, you stopped caring about me. Did you forget I'm your mother? I gave you everything, and now you've left me in the dust for some..." She hesitates, a venomous pause before adding, "some gold digger."

Ferris can't hold back his tone anymore—and at this point, he doesn't even try. "That's it!" he erupts, his voice shaking with fury. "You can't see that you're ruining everything—every relationship around you. I'm done with this. Done with you."

He stops to take a breath, trying to steady himself. "I can't believe it's come to this, but you can keep your wedding invitation. We don't want you there anymore." His voice sharpens, "And that's *my* decision—not Sloan's. So don't you dare blame her. I'm done."

Without another word, Ferris slams the phone down, throwing it violently against the wall. The sound of it shattering echoes through the room, a loud, final punctuation to everything that's just been said.

Sloan hears the crash from the other room. Heart pounding, she slowly pushes open the bedroom door and peeks inside, checking to see if Ferris is still on the phone. When she sees him sitting on the bed, head buried in his hands, she steps in.

"Fer, what's going on?"

She crosses the room carefully, sinking onto the bed beside him. Her hand finds his back, a gentle, grounding touch.

Ferris lifts his head slightly, his eyes heavy with frustration. He starts to speak, but instead, he exhales sharply, raking a hand through his hair.

Without a word, Sloan moves her hand to the back of his neck, giving it a firm, reassuring squeeze, hoping to ease even a fraction of the tension weighing on him.

He closes his eyes and strokes his chin with his thumb and forefinger. "Well, I just uninvited my mom from the wedding," Sloan looks like she's going to speak, but instead leans back to listen, her eyes wide. "She played victim again the whole time on the phone. Turns out she's in Siesta Key and is taking her anger out on me...us, like usual. I'm just sick of the way she treats you. I'm sick of the victim mode she always is in. I'm so over all the drama. I just want to enjoy this time in my life and all I'm doing is wondering what issue will come up next."

Sloan looks at him confused, her eyes squinting at him to try to understand better. Did he really just say he uninvited his mom? She always thought about this but never thought it would actually happen. If this is what she always wanted, why does she feel so unsatisfied? "Woah. That's a lot to take in," she pauses, "Wait, did you say your mom was in Siesta Key? What's she doing there?"

Ferris shakes his head in shame, "Yeah, apparently, she's there to crash your bachelorette party, go figure, but Jenny purposely told her the wrong address because she wouldn't take no for an answer. She tried to put all the blame on you saying she paid for the bachelorette party and that you never actually invited her." Ferris stands up from the bed to pick up his phone that's lying in the corner of the room.

Sloan is still piecing everything together, and suddenly, it all clicks. "Oh my gosh... that's why Jenny said to thank your mom after the trip."

At the time, she truly believed it was his mom finally understanding and respecting her boundaries. But now, it's clear—it wasn't Kate at all. It was Jenny, quietly shielding her, playing defense in a way only someone who knew Kate too well could.

It felt harsh, but sometimes that was the only way to get through to people like Kate. And even though Sloan had no part in it, she already knew—somehow, it would still be her fault.

Chapter 21

Jenny finds herself doom scrolling anxiously on her phone. Her hair is pulled up in a messy bun, and she's wearing her favorite Chappell Roan hoodie with black leggings. Exhausted from the trip, she's soaking in the last few hours of freedom before another busy week of work and school. She has a big paper due at the end of the month on *Family Dynamics and Emotional Boundaries*—which, ironically, feels a little too on the nose. She starts to wonder if her real life could count as internship credits for her degree.

She figures her unpaid internship must be starting a little early when her mom's name pops up on her phone. Hesitantly, she answers—half dreading it, half ready to put her schooling into practice.

Before the phone even makes it to her ear Kate starts yelling on the other side of the phone, "You take my money, you lie to me about where you're going, act like I'm invited, and then hang up on me in the airport? What the hell is wrong with you?!" There's a loud pound like Kate might have slammed her fist into a table.

Jenny is lying back on the couch, head on a pillow, and her phone, now on speaker, is lying on her chest. She responds calmly, "One, I didn't take your money. You gave it to me willingly. Did I use it for something different? Sure. But you did pay for your hotel with it. Two, I only lied to you because you weren't taking no for an answer, and three, I never once acted like you were invited. You kept pushing and I said I would talk to Sloan." Even though Kate isn't talking, Jenny can hear her breathing. Kate's in full panic mode that the walls around her are closing in and she's losing control. "By the sound of it, you could probably use a little R&R. I couldn't think of a better place to do it than Siesta Key at a little swanky hotel. So, you're welcome."

Kate is walking around the hotel room, lifting up the sofa to make sure the place isn't infested. "Well, I'm doing anything but relaxing right now. Thanks to you!" The sarcasm is clear, but everything else is a little wishy-washy. She makes her way to the bathroom and notices a smudge on the mirror. She takes a towel and starts wiping it profusely.

"Come on, Mom, when's the last time you took a vacation by yourself? Why don't you put on some sunscreen, grab a good book, and go read by the beach? It will be good for you. Get a nice little base tan before the wedding."

Silence and then a sniffle, "I just got uninvited to Ferris and Sloan's wedding, again, all thanks to you." Kate's voice grows louder.

Jenny sighs, pressing the phone against her ear as she leans back on the couch. "Oh, Mother. Sweet, sweet Mother," she says with mock sympathy. "You made your bed a long time ago."

Her mom scoffs on the other end, demanding to know exactly what her money paid for. Jenny calmly lays it out—Sloan's upgrade to first class, and the limo to the airport—both of which were thoroughly enjoyed. And of course, she paid for her own hotel room. *Now wasn't that nice?*

That, of course, wasn't what her mom had intended—and now she expects to be paid back.

Jenny raises an eyebrow. *Does she really want me to go around asking the bride and bridesmaids for reimbursements? Wouldn't she rather save face after everything?*

But her mom huffs, bitter and unmoved. "I'm already uninvited to the wedding, so what's the point now?"

"Right," Jenny says, her voice dry. "You are. And demanding your money back would only make you look even pettier. But if you let them keep it and tell Sloan it was a gift—that you really wanted her to enjoy her bachelorette party—then you're leaving on a high note. Wouldn't you like to do something selflessly for Ferris and Sloan?"

There's a long pause on the other end of the line. Jenny can almost hear her mom clenching her jaw.

After some back-and-forth, her mom finally agrees—grudgingly—to forget about the money for the bachelorette, take some time to relax, and start to make peace with the fact that she won't be at the wedding.

But just before hanging up, her voice sharpens again. "But you can tell Ferris and Sloan... I won't forgive them."

Jenny exhales, about to respond, when her phone buzzes with a new text from Sloan that now Callum's no longer coming to the wedding.

She groans, rubbing her forehead. Ferris just can't catch a break. "Okay, Mom. Get outside, enjoy the beach," she says, already mentally shifting into damage-control mode. She hangs up and immediately starts dialing Ferris, ready to figure out what the hell is going on now.

***

Jenny felt like she was living in Grand Central Station. From the moment she walked back through her front door after the bachelorette party, it had been nonstop drama. She had just gotten off the phone with Ferris, calling him the second she heard that Callum was stepping down from the wedding. Callum had been his best friend since they were kids, so it was shocking that he would drop out of the wedding for some girl he practically just met.

Between everything with their mom and now Callum, Jenny knew Ferris had to be overwhelmed. He loved Sloan—there was no question—but the constant chaos leading up to the wedding had drained so much of the joy from it. She reminded him why they wanted to get married in the first place—that none of the outside drama mattered. And if they needed to block everyone out and focus on each other, then that's exactly what they should do.

On the other side of town, Ferris is sitting in his office when he hangs up the phone with Jenny. Talking to her really put everything into perspective. They are putting together this huge wedding. It's been non-stop drama from the start and it's taking away the real meaning of the marriage. He wanted to shake off the stress and step into their next chapter the way it was meant to be—relaxed and excited.

He knew what they needed to do. He quickly stands up from his desk, throws his phone in his back pocket, and bolts into the kitchen, where Sloan is warming up some leftovers.

Sloan hears him coming down the hall and quickly turns around. "Well, you've had a change in demeanor. What are you looking all excited about?"

Ferris scoots closer to Sloan and puts his arms around her shoulders. "So, I just got off the phone with Jenny, and I've been thinking. We've been so focused on making everyone happy around us and it's really taking away from our wedding. I'm so stressed thinking about that day and I can tell you are too. There's so much pressure about this big moment and everything being perfect," he turns to the fridge where their invitation is posted up with a magnet and gestures towards it.

Sloan looks at him like she's trying to figure him out. "I mean, yeah, you're not wrong. But what are you trying to say?"

Ferris zooms back in close to her and throws one arm around her shoulder. "What if we just got away?"

Sloan steps back, confused. "What do you mean, what if we just got away? We've got a wedding in 3 weeks," she says gesturing back to their invitation on the refrigerator.

"I know, I know and we won't miss that," he pauses and looks to the right like he's thinking of a plan right then and there. "What if we take off to a beach for a vacation—just the two of us—and don't tell anyone?"

Sloan isn't buying it. Ferris has a plan, like always. She squints at him and puts her hand on her chin, "What are you *really* thinking, Ferris?"

He pulls his lips in and smiles, like he's trying to hold back from saying something wild—and then he blurts it out. "I'm thinking... we go on this vacation and maybe, just maybe, while we're there—we get married?"

He sees Sloan's hesitation but keeps going. "I mean, you said it yourself in the beginning—you just wanted something small. And now it's turned into this huge, chaotic thing with drama, my mom, the whole Callum situation... it's all just noise at this point. I don't want to lose sight of what really matters. I want to protect that—protect us."

And suddenly, it's like something clicks. Sloan isn't swept up in a fantasy—she's just... tired. Tired of the drama, the endless planning, the fights, the people-pleasing. She pictures their wedding day—quiet, simple, just the two of them on a beach. No interruptions. No expectations. Just love and a fresh start.

She lets out a breath and wraps her arms around Ferris's waist. "I mean, when you put it that way... yeah. It's been a lot. And doing something just for us—no stress, no audience—honestly sounds like the best decision we've made in months."

Ferris immediately pulls his phone from his back pocket and starts clicking away. "So what do you say? We book a flight, get married, and figure the rest out later?"

Sloan laughs, but it's the kind of laugh that comes with relief. "Okay, this is a little crazy... but yes. I'm in."

They immediately dive into planning and getting plane tickets. Since their wedding was in less than a month, they didn't have time to wait. While talking, they quickly realized that eloping didn't feel right if it meant leaving out the people they loved most. Sloan couldn't imagine getting married without her mom there, and after everything Jenny had done for them, they knew she had to be part of it too. To avoid losing their wedding deposit, they decided to scrap the ceremony and turn it into a big reception instead, cutting costs where they could. The reality of their decision started to sink in, but Sloan was all in, and Ferris made sure she had the final say.

Chapter 22

As Jenny presses the phone to her ear, she can hear the sound of waves crashing and the faint chatter of people in the background. "Hey, Mom, just wanted to check in. Are you enjoying your vacation?"

"Well, it's not terrible," her mom replies, her voice warm but a little forced. "The beach is... nice, although I realized how much I hate sand, so I've been hanging around the pool."

Jenny smirks, picturing her mom in a beach chair with a fruity drink in one hand and a judgmental text halfway typed in the other. "That good, huh?"

"Better than I thought. But I'm still not very happy with you, so don't get it twisted." She pauses, her tone shifting just slightly. "I tried yoga on the beach—though the instructor clearly thinks I'm eighty." A short, slightly self-deprecating laugh followed. "And I found a café that serves the best key lime pie I've ever had. Way better than the dessert at Sloan's bridal shower."

Jenny rolls her eyes, already bracing herself. "That sounds like a dream," she says carefully. "So, you're coming home tomorrow, right?"

Her mom hesitates. "Actually... I'm staying for a few more days. Dad's flying in to join me."

Jenny's eyebrows shoot up. "Wow, that's great! You must really be loving it there."

"I wouldn't say love... but what else am I supposed to do? No one at home wants me around," she says, almost surprised by the words. Her tone shifts—still casual, but not quite comfortable. "Anyway, Jen, I don't have much time—I've got bingo at six—but before I go, I just wanted to say..."

A pause.

"I've been thinking a lot about this wedding. About... everything. And I think I really need to do something. I can't imagine not seeing Ferris get married. And I can see now that I wasn't as welcoming to Sloan as I should have been." Another pause. "But I mean, they *have* put me in a difficult position."

Jenny blinks in surprise, ignoring the last comment—*classic Mom*. This was the last thing she expected to hear. "Mom..."

"I know, I know," she sighs. "I don't even know what I was trying to prove, but I see now that I've only made things worse. Maybe it's time I try to make things right."

Jenny swallows the lump in her throat. Maybe this vacation really had started to change her mom.

"So, I actually just sent them this beautiful fruit basket with a note explaining how sorry I am. I told them I hope they can understand and accept my apology, but if they don't, that's okay."

"Wow. Well, color me impressed—sounds like the beach has changed you, Mom." Jenny shares her surprise, although beneath the surface she's still suspicious.

Just then, a faint knock startles her. She pulls the phone away from her ear while her mom continues to talk, her eyes fixed on the door. She wasn't expecting anyone—Ferris would have mentioned it if he was coming over.

The mystery person knocks again.

"Um, hey Mom, I gotta go—someone's at the door."

Her mom quickly says goodbye, and Jenny slowly walks over to answer it, creeping toward the door, tilting her head to peek out the front window to see who could possibly be there. All she can make out is the silhouette of a man standing on her front step. She knows better than to answer the door for a strange man empty-handed, so she quickly grabs a baseball bat from her front closet.

She slowly wraps her fingers around the knob and starts to turn.

"Jenny? It's me." The panicked, familiar voice makes her freeze. She pulls the door open, and there he is—Callum. Standing there like a lost puppy with nowhere to go.

He's wearing a dark gray baseball hat, a hunter-green hoodie, and jeans. His hair is tousled, and the lenses of his glasses are slightly smudged. "Can I come in?" he asks, his voice edged with something Jenny can't quite place.

Jenny doesn't realize she is holding her breath until she lets it out in a sharp exhale. "Callum, what the hell are you doing here?"

Callum rubs the back of his neck, turning away as if he isn't sure he should be there at all. "Look, I'm sorry for showing up unannounced, but can I come in for a second?"

Without a word, Jenny pulls the door open wider and holds out one arm as if to gesture for him to step inside. He hesitates before walking in, his gaze sweeping the room—then landing on the baseball bat still clutched in her other hand.

"Do you always answer the door with a baseball bat?" His eyes flick from the bat to Jenny's face as she shuts the door behind him.

"No. Just when unexpected men I don't recognize show up," she shoots back, walking into the kitchen to grab her water bottle. She takes a sip before leveling him with a look. "So, what brings you by? Wanted to tell me in person that you bailed on my brother's wedding?" She shakes her head with a dry laugh.

"No," Callum sighs. "I figured you already heard about that through the grapevine. I didn't bail, but I know I messed up and I need to fix it." He pulls his phone from his pocket, sets it on the table and spins it with his fingertips, a nervous habit.

Jenny folds her arms. "Fix it?" she repeats. "Do you have any idea how much stress Ferris is under right now? Everything with my mom, and now you—his best friend. You were supposed to be there for him, and you completely let him down." She grabs the sweatshirt draped over the couch, pulling it on before plopping down with a sigh. "So, I'll ask again—why are you even here?"

Callum hesitates before speaking. He walks over to join her in the living room, but he doesn't sit down. He uncomfortably stands in the front of the room as if he's giving Jenny a small presentation. "Gretchen and I got into a huge fight. We broke up. I tried kicking her out, but she said she needed one more night, and I had nowhere else to go. I panicked and I showed up here." He exhales as if he's been holding onto that for a while.

Jenny sits up in her seat realizing this is going to be a much more complicated conversation. "So, you showed up here because you have no one else since you burned bridges with my brother?"

Callum steps closer and starts to sit on the arm of the couch. "Jenny, you know you aren't my last resort. I could really use a good friend right now," he looks deep into her eyes.

Jenny starts picking at her nails, "I'll listen, but that's it. I've already chosen my side. You know I'm going to be backing my brother up."

"I'm not asking you to take sides. In fact, none of this is about Ferris. I was completely blinded by Gretchen." He's now sitting on the couch with Jenny and puts his palm to his forehead.

"Yeah, you really know how to pick them. So, what happened anyway?"

Callum admits that Ferris had been helping him with bills for months since Gretchen and Christy moved in, leaving him to cover everything on his own. Too afraid to speak up about not being able to afford it, he'd let it go—until Ferris let it slip to Gretchen. Embarrassed and angry, she lashed out, and their relationship fell apart.

As he explains everything, Jenny can't help but point out the real issue: he'd been willing to drop out of his best friend's wedding for a girl who had clearly been using him. Callum insists that he never actually would have gone through with it, but Jenny isn't sure she believes him.

"Bluff or not, I don't think you're invited anymore."

Callum's face falls. "What do you mean? I can make it up to him. He hasn't been a perfect friend either."

"You literally just went on about how Ferris has been helping you pay bills while you lied to your girlfriend. I don't think you can blame Ferris for not being a perfect friend. Ferris and Sloan are just over it." Jenny hesitates before adding, "So, did you come all the way here just to talk about your breakup? Because I'm not sure I can listen to much more of this, honestly."

Callum exhales, rubbing the back of his neck. "I'm sorry. You're probably right. You were just the first person that popped into my mind. Ferris doesn't want to see me right now, and I figured you'd get me. I thought maybe you'd know what I should do."

Jenny glances down at her lap, wondering when she became everyone's unpaid therapist. When she looks back up, she forces a small smile. "Well, one thing I wouldn't do is show up at my ex's house right after getting dumped."

Callum chuckles, shaking his head. "Okay, well, *technically* I didn't break up with her. She kind of broke up with me." He exhales and looks away before adding, "But yeah, I know—you're right. It's weird, and I'm putting you in an awkward position." His voice softens as he glances at her. "I know we dated a long time ago, but I guess I still always thought of you as a friend."

The words hang between them, heavier than he probably intended. Jenny isn't sure if she believes him, or if she even wants to.

Suddenly, as if realizing how misplaced he is, Callum pushes off the couch, stepping back toward the table where his phone sits. "I don't know what I was thinking."

Without thinking, Jenny starts to get up from the couch and step towards him, "It's fine. But you have to make this right. You can't keep depending on everyone to fix your problems." She walks up to him and pats him on the shoulder.

Callum glances over at her, his tone light but teasing. "Careful, Jen. You know what happened last time you touched me like that."

Jenny quickly pulls her hand back, a little flustered. "Okay, don't make it weird now. I'm still very pissed off at you."

Just then, her phone starts buzzing on the kitchen counter, cutting through the moment. She quickly steps away from Callum, almost as if caught doing something she shouldn't be, and walks over to grab the phone. Glancing at the screen, she says, "Hold on, Ferris is calling me," before looking up at Callum and placing the phone to her ear.

"Hey, Ferris. Is everything okay? What's going on?"

"Jenny! Yes, everything's amazing. I'm at the airport, and I'm here with Sloan." A voice in the background interrupts, "Jenny, pack your bags. We're eloping!"

Part 6

Chapter 23

"You're eloping?" Jenny presses the phone to her ear, nodding along to Sloan's excited voice, but her eyes flicker to Callum beside her. Her brows lift as if to ask, *Should I step outside?* She purses her lips, only half-processing what Sloan is saying, tilting her head in question as she debates whether or not to be more discreet.

"What do you mean you're eloping?!" Jenny's voice rises. *"When I said to block everyone out, I didn't mean disappear and get married out of nowhere!"*

Ferris starts to respond, but Sloan pulls the phone back toward her mouth. "Well, it started as just a relaxing weekend away, and the more we talked about it, the more we realized...we'd rather have a small, intimate wedding."

Ferris leans into the speaker. "Yeah, and we'll do the big party later on our original wedding date. But this way, we get the wedding we actually want—no drama, no distractions." As he speaks, he glances at Sloan, trailing her luggage through the airport check-in line beside him.

Jenny thinks about it for a moment and looks over at Callum, who looks more than confused. He's feeling like he's listening in on a conversation he shouldn't be a part of. "You know, I think it's a great idea!"

Callum smiles along with her, not sure what this means for him, but he's happy to be a part of it.

"Great! Because we want you to be there with us when we get married!" Sloan says through the speaker as she throws her hair up into a high ponytail. "So hurry up and just get here! The flight leaves in two hours, and there's still room on the plane."

As Sloan adjusts the straps of her carry-on, Ferris glances up at the departure board to make sure they're not missing anything. She gives him a quick smile, but her attention is divided as she scrolls through her phone. A new message from her mom pops up, letting her know she's at the airport and will meet them at the gate.

Jenny looks around, unsure how she's going to pack, drive to the airport, and make the flight in time. But if she didn't at least try, she'd regret it. She immediately runs toward the front door, opens her closet, and starts rummaging for a bag.

Callum walks over by her and helps pull out the duffle Jenny gestures toward. She laughs at how ridiculous and awesome this is. "Alright, I'm about to hit the record for the fastest packer in the world," she says, grabbing the duffle. She heads toward her room, but stops and looks back at Callum. "Wait, um, guys, I'm not alone right now."

Ferris and Sloan have checked in and are now making their way over to the security line. "Who are you with?" he asks Jenny, looking confused. "Oh, is it that guy Charlie you're seeing? Bring him along! I mean, as long as he's no drama, bring him. But anyways, Jenny, we're heading into security now, so I gotta hang up. We'll see you guys soon!"

Jenny ends the call with Ferris, her fingers still gripping the phone a little too tightly. Her heart pounds, a mix of urgency and anxiety flooding through her as she turns on her heel and rushes into her bedroom. She flings open her dresser drawers, grabbing whatever she can—socks, shirts, a pair of jeans she hopes are clean—and shoves them into her duffel bag without a second thought.

Her mind is already at the airport, already in the next few hours ahead. The whole ordeal with Ferris has pushed everything else out of her mind, including the fact that she wasn't alone in the apartment.

Callum stands by the doorway, hands stuffed into his pockets, watching the storm of motion unravel in front of him. He shifts his weight from one foot to the other, clearing his throat as if to remind her that he's still there. But Jenny doesn't even look up. She darts into the bathroom, yanks open the cabinet, and tosses a handful of toiletries into the bag—half of them probably unnecessary.

Callum exhales sharply, biting his lip. What now? He knew Jenny well enough to know she wouldn't want him hanging around while she was gone. They hadn't even really figured out what was happening between them, and this wasn't the time to have that conversation.

"Jenny—" he starts, but she zips up the duffel bag so hard the sound practically slices through the air.

"Ah, there's so much to do," she says quickly, running in front of him through to the kitchen. Then, suddenly, she stops. "What are you just staring at me for?"

"So, uh... I guess you're going on a trip," Callum blurts out, not sure what else to say.

"Don't you mean *we*?" Jenny shoots back.

Callum furrows his brows and quickly shakes his head. "No, no. Ferris definitely doesn't want me there. I'll just...uh—" He grabs his phone off the table, shoves it into his pocket, and starts toward the front door.

Before he can leave, Jenny swiftly steps in front of him, placing her hands on his shoulders to turn him back toward her. She locks eyes with him and says firmly, "Stop. You're coming with me. I can't imagine Ferris wanting to get married without you. I know things got out of hand, but you guys are brothers. The toxicity is gone—you can repair this."

***

By some miracle, Jenny and Callum make it to the airport with about thirty minutes to spare. They had decided not to let Ferris know Callum was coming. This way, they could let Sloan and

Ferris continue their wedded bliss, and when Jenny found them at the gate, it would be a little surprise.

On the way, Jenny called Ferris to find out what flight they needed to book and get all the details of this spontaneous trip. Ferris excitedly told her they were getting married at the Grand Canyon and would be flying into Flagstaff, Arizona.

Callum sits quietly beside her, staring out the window, wondering if he's made the right decision. The past twenty-four hours had been a whirlwind—one chaotic moment after another. He'd gotten into a huge fight with Ferris, broken up with his girlfriend, and then, for some reason, let her and her daughter stay at his apartment overnight. He half-expected his phone to light up with desperate calls or messages, but surprisingly, it remained silent. It started seeming meant to be though, because if it weren't for him running out of the house and over to Jenny's, he never would have heard about the elopement or had a bag ready to go in his car.

As soon as they step into the airport, the reality of what they are doing sets in. Jenny quickly pulls up their mobile boarding passes—luckily, she had enough flight points to cover Callum's flight too—and they scan their tickets at the kiosk before rushing toward security. The TSA line is mercifully short, but the pressure of the ticking clock makes every second stretch unbearably long.

Jenny hastily slips off her shoes and tosses them into a bin, along with her carry-on bag, before stepping through the scanner. Callum follows suit, barely catching his balance as he tugs off his boots.

The TSA agent barely glances at them as they grab their things and take off, practically jogging toward their gate. Jenny keeps her eyes locked on the terminal signs, her heart racing. "There it is! Gate 24," she says, pointing ahead.

As they get closer, she spots Ferris and Sloan sitting together, completely in their own world. Sloan's mom is sitting across from them, legs crossed, flipping through a magazine. Sloan is animatedly talking, while Ferris listens with a soft grin.

They start to turn in that direction but then Jenny comes up with an idea. She urges Callum to stop over at the kiosk nearby to let her have a head start and warm them up to the idea. Callum agrees and walks over to the kiosk to browse some hats.

As Jenny starts walking over, Ferris spots her and immediately nudges Sloan as they stand up from their chairs. "Jenny, you made it!" Ferris says as he throws his hands up in an excited gesture. Sloan runs in for a hug then quickly backs up and turns to pull her mom in.

"You remember my mom, Virginia," Sloan smiles at her mom. "She's coming too!"

Virginia smiles wide, her long summer dress flowing as she leans in. "Hi, Jenny, great seeing you again," she reaches up and touches Jenny's arm. "It's my first time to the Grand Canyon. I cannot wait!"

Sloan gestures for Jenny to follow her back to their seats. Once they settle in, Jenny drops her bag onto the floor and sits beside her.

Sloan exhales happily. "Jenny, I'm so glad you're here. I don't know why we didn't do this from the start. I feel amazing—so excited."

"I'm glad you guys are excited! I feel like this is the first time you're really doing something for yourselves." She leans around making it clear she's talking to both Ferris and Sloan. "So, what made you decide on The Grand Canyon?"

Ferris takes a sip from his water bottle before setting it down beside him. "We thought about a beach wedding, but it felt a little cliché. The mountains, though? You just can't beat that view in the photos."

"Wow, that sounds incredible." Jenny smiles, but her attention shifts past Sloan as she spots Callum approaching. He's moving slowly, waiting for some kind of signal from her before coming any closer.

Sloan notices Jenny making a face at someone behind her and quickly turns to look.

Ferris starts to say, "So, I take it you decided to leave Charlie at home? Because I could've sworn you said *we* when you called me from the car."

Jenny flashes a nervous smile. "I did say *we*, but it's not Charlie. He's long out of my life."

Ferris furrows his brows in confusion, but before he can respond, Sloan spots Callum walking toward them and quickly taps Ferris's arm.

"Okay, so who's this mystery man?" Ferris asks, still focused on Jenny.

"Uh, hey, Ferris." Callum approaches hesitantly, shifting his backpack over one shoulder, his other hand stuffed in his pocket.

Ferris turns sharply, his expression hardening as his gaze lands on Callum. "You've got to be kidding me." He stands up, looking between Jenny and Callum, his frustration mounting. "This was supposed to be a stress-free trip. You're *literally* one of the reasons we wanted to elope. Why the hell did you think it was okay to show up?"

Callum falters, glancing at Jenny, silently pleading for backup.

Jenny quickly stands, placing a steady hand on Ferris's shoulder. "Okay, look—he wasn't going to come. I *made* him. I know you've been under a lot of stress, and trust me, I wouldn't have encouraged him if I didn't think you'd regret it later."

Ferris's jaw clenches, anger flashing in his eyes, but he doesn't cut her off. He trusts Jenny—even if he doesn't like what she's saying.

She softens her voice. "Callum and Gretchen broke up. She's out of the picture."

Ferris's eyebrows lift slightly at this. He doesn't say anything, but Jenny can see the shift—the light at the end of the tunnel.

Callum takes a cautious step forward, noticing Ferris's gaze beginning to soften. "Yeah, Ferris, look... I know I really screwed up. And I'm sorry. I let things go south way too fast, and that's on me. You've always had my back, covered for me when I needed it, and I should have done the same for you."

Ferris exhales sharply like he's about to say something, but he hesitates. Instead, he just watches Callum, letting him speak.

Callum swallows hard. "I went to Jenny's because I had nowhere else to go. I was there when you called, and she really encouraged me to come. But if you tell me right now that you don't want me here, I get it. I'll turn around and go home. The last thing I want is to make things worse."

Ferris studies Callum's face carefully. His words are adding up, but there's still a nagging voice in the back of his mind, making him hesitate. He glances at Sloan, who has been quietly observing the whole exchange. She's seated cross-legged in her chair, idly spinning the ring on her finger—a nervous habit Ferris noticed since they got engaged. Her brows are slightly furrowed as if she's deep in thought, but when she catches Ferris looking at her, she flashes him a wide, reassuring smile, the kind that silently says, *It's going to be okay.*

Ferris exhales and looks back at Callum. "Okay, well, I don't know if it's the whiskey and Coke I had when I got to the airport or what you're saying to me, but I think that was a pretty good apology." He glances back at Sloan. "What do you think?"

Sloan stops fiddling with her ring and tilts her head, pretending to ponder the question. Then, with a playful smirk, she winks at Ferris before turning to face Callum. "Alright, alright. You can come. But I swear, if I hear the name *Gretchen* come out of your mouth even once on this trip, you're done."

Callum laughs lightly, holding his hands up in surrender. "Understood."

Satisfied, Sloan gets up from her seat and wraps her arms around Callum in a brief but firm hug, officially welcoming him onto the trip. The moment is short-lived, though, as the gate attendant's voice crackles over the speakers, announcing pre-boarding.

The five of them shuffle into line, scanning their boarding passes before stepping onto the jet bridge. Ferris and Sloan lead the way, with Virginia following close behind, clutching her oversized tote like it contains state secrets. Jenny and Callum trail just behind her.

Once onboard, they settle into their seats. Sloan, Ferris, and Virginia sit together, while Jenny and Callum take seats a few rows back. As they reach their row, Callum grabs Jenny's duffle bag and effortlessly hoists it into the overhead compartment. She slips into her seat, adjusting the fabric of her shirt and buckling her seatbelt as she settles in. After tossing his own bag up next to hers, Callum takes a seat beside her, giving a quick glance out the window as the plane begins to fill up.

As the plane takes off, Virginia leans back in her chair, already half asleep, while Sloan presses her forehead against the window, watching the city lights shrink beneath them. "I can't believe we're actually doing this," she murmurs, her breath fogging up the glass.

Ferris chuckles, stretching his legs out as much as the cramped space allows. He reaches over to her lap, his fingers gently wrapping around her thigh. "Really? I can." He leans over and places a soft kiss on her forehead.

After a smooth flight, the plane touches down in Flagstaff, the small airport buzzing with the quiet energy of travelers coming and going. As they step off the jet bridge and into the terminal, Virginia lets out a contented sigh, stretching her arms. "Well, that was a lovely flight! I still can't believe we're here for a wedding. This is just wonderful," she says, beaming at Sloan and Ferris.

Ferris grabs their carry-on bags while Sloan links her arm through her mom's. "Thanks for coming, Mom. It means so much to have you here."

"Oh, sweetheart, of course! There's nowhere else I'd rather be." Virginia pats her daughter's hand and glances over at Jenny and Callum. "And I have to say, this is quite the adventure! Now, let's get you two married in style."

The group makes their way toward baggage claim, the excitement settling in as the crisp Arizona air greets them outside. Sloan takes a deep breath, letting it all in—this time, it feels like the beginning of something good.

Chapter 24

The next day, Sloan wakes up to sunlight peeking through her windows. She and Ferris had decided to keep it traditional and spend the night before the wedding apart. The scent of fresh coffee wafts through the air, and she takes a deep breath while stretching before opening her eyes.

Jenny, who slept on the pull-out couch, has been up for an hour already, reading on the balcony, sipping coffee, and preparing breakfast. She wanted to make sure Sloan felt every bit of the bridal excitement, even though they were away from most of their family and friends.

Noticing that Sloan is up, Jenny gets up from her spot and walks to the coffee bar to pour a cup for Sloan, adding just a splash of cream, exactly how she likes it. She returned to where Sloan is sitting, pulling on a sweatshirt.

"Happy Wedding Day, Sloan!" Jenny smiles brightly as she hands over the coffee. "I hope you slept well—it's going to be a busy morning!"

Jenny walks back to the breakfast bar, tossing a bagel in the toaster and arranging some fruit on a plate.

Sloan takes a sip of her coffee, eyeing Jenny with a raised brow. "Jenny, I told you not to do anything crazy. We're just having a simple exchange of vows. That's it." She tosses the covers off and joins Jenny at the counter, grabbing a piece of fruit.

"I know, I know. I just thought you might want to remember this day," Jenny says with a playful smirk.

Just then, there's a knock at the door. Sloan jumps up, calling out, "Oh! That must be my mom. I told her to come by when she woke up." She opens the door, only to step back in surprise. It was indeed her mom, but she wasn't alone.

Behind her stood three women, each carrying equipment.

"Morning, ladies!" Virginia greets cheerfully. "I was in the elevator and ran into these wonderful women on their way up!"

Sloan's face shifts to one of confusion as she hugs her mom.

Jenny quickly turns around and smiles. "Ah, yes! You must be the photographer, makeup artist, and hairstylist! Right this way, please!" She floats over to the window-side table, gesturing for them to set up there.

Sloan, still holding her bagel, throws a look over her shoulder. "Jenny, what is all this?"

"Every bride deserves to feel like a princess on her day," Jenny says with a grin, grabbing a bottle of champagne and pouring. "I did some last-minute research yesterday at the airport and, luckily, they had availability to take care of you today!" She hands a glass of champagne to Virginia.

Virginia takes the glass but pauses before sipping. "Oh honey, it's 8 a.m. Way too early for that," she says, walking over to the counter to grab the orange juice. She pours a splash into her glass and takes a sip. "Much better!"

***

Meanwhile, Ferris has just gotten out of the shower and is drying off when he hears his phone ding that he got a text. He opens the phone to see a text from his mom.

Hi Ferris, just wanted to say I've sent something to your home. That's it. No need to thank me.

He suddenly has a pit in his stomach and starts to feel bad for not inviting her. But then that moment quickly goes away when he gets a second text.

Well, a thank you would be nice, especially from Sloan. I mean, you can't ignore me forever. I would really appreciate being included in your day after everything you've put me through.

He throws his phone down on the bed. He should have left it at home and relied on the hotel phone. But he wasn't going to let his mom in his head anymore. He needed to be fully present for Sloan, who would officially be his new family after today.

A few hours later, Sloan, Jenny, and her mom have hair and makeup completed, a mini get-ready photo shoot, and the flowers have been dropped off. They are finally headed out to meet Ferris and Callum at the site for the vow exchange. Ferris found a private location with a stunning view of the canyon behind them.

As they pull up in the car they see Ferris, Callum, and the Officiant chatting in the distance. Ferris is nervously swaying with his hands in his pockets, while Callum keeps running his hands through his hair.

Jenny and Virginia head over to the spot first so Sloan can make her grand entrance. Sloan walks up smiling and the way the sun is shining she almost looks like an angel. Sloan's white dress is effortlessly romantic, perfect for an intimate elopement. The soft fabric hugs her waist before flowing into a billowy skirt that brushes against her knees.

The square neckline frames her collarbones, and delicate buttons trail down the bodice, adding just the right amount of detail. It was the kind of dress that felt both timeless and spontaneous—a representation of their love story. Her sleeves, slightly puffed at the shoulders, gives the dress a touch of vintage charm, balancing elegance with a carefree spirit. Her hair is in loose curls flowing just past her shoulders, and she has a thin gold tiara for an effortless touch of elegance, adding a hint of whimsy to her bridal look. Ferris can hardly catch his breath.

As Sloan approaches the front of the altar, which is more or less a small podium, Ferris nervously smiles wide and whispers, "You are gorgeous."

"Welcome, everyone, and thank you for joining me today. My name is Jackie Tyler and I'm here to officiate this beautiful wedding of Ferris Hayes and Sloan Bartels," she throws her hands out as if she's speaking for a large audience, even though there are only five in front of her.

"Ferris, do you take Sloan to be your lawfully wedded wife?"

Ferris takes no time to answer, squeezing Sloan's hands. "I do."

Jackie continues, "And Sloan, do you take Ferris to be your lawfully wedded husband?"

Sloan squeezes right back, "I do."

"Wonderful! By the power vested in me, I now introduce for the very first time, Mr. and Mrs. Ferris and Sloan Hayes. You may kiss your bride!" Jackie raises both her hands up as Ferris pulls Sloan in and spins to dip her for a long, romantic kiss.

Jenny, Callum, and Virginia cheer and clap loudly. Jackie congratulates them again before the photographer takes a few posed photos in front of the canyon. They head to a picnic table to sign the marriage license. They give their thanks and goodbye to Jackie as the five of them head out to grab a late lunch to celebrate.

When the host takes them to their table, Jenny orders a bottle of champagne to get the celebrations going right away. Sloan walks up and as she plops down in the booth, the airy material on her dress fans out around her, settling in gentle waves.

Ferris follows immediately behind her still in awe of her beauty. He always is, but today was something different. Maybe it was the beauty of the day, them doing something for themselves for once, the excitement for the next chapter of their lives beginning, or a mixture of it all.

The server comes back with a bottle of champagne and five glasses, and all their attention is immediately turned as she pops the bottle and begins to pour. As the server walks away, Jenny picks up her fork and does a quiet "clink" onto her glass.

"If you guys don't mind, I'd like to say a few words." Jenny looks directly at Ferris and Sloan. They share a smile before nodding, giving her the go-ahead. She takes a breath, then lets out a small laugh. "I told myself I wouldn't cry," she says, glancing down as if giving herself a pep talk before looking back up. "But here we are."

Her eyes soften as she continues. "From the moment Ferris first brought you home, Sloan, I knew you were the one. Not just because of the way you love him, but because of the way you bring out the best in each other. You challenge one another, support one another, and somehow, in the middle of life's chaos, you make each other stronger.

No matter what's been thrown your way, you've never wavered. You've faced every challenge together and come out even more unshakable. If that's any sign of what's ahead, I know you're in for a lifetime of happiness."

A tear escapes down her cheek, but she doesn't wipe it away. She simply smiles. "I admire you both so much, and I will always be rooting for you."

She lifts her glass. "Alright, before I turn into a complete mess—cheers!"

They all reach up with their glasses and click, while Ferris quickly turns to Sloan and gives her a peck on the lips. Sloan kisses him back and turns to look at Jenny, "Thank you, Jenny! That really means a lot to us. We're so grateful for your support through all of this. I really don't know how we would have done it without you."

Virginia quietly smiles at the group, she's just happy to be a part of the celebration.

Callum, feeling a mix of gratitude and redemption, lifts his glass with a small smile. "Yeah, what she said. Congrats, you two. And... thanks for letting me be here after everything. It means more than you know." He exhales, glancing between them. "How do you guys feel?"

Ferris turns to Sloan, his eyes full of love. "Amazing."

Sloan nods, squeezing his hand. "Best decision ever. Yeah, I feel pretty amazing."

They settle into their lunch, surrounded by great people, soaking in the beauty of the day and enjoying a rare, drama-free moment. After the meal, as they start heading back to the hotel, Sloan pulls Jenny aside.

"Hey, so... Jenny, I want to talk to you for a sec."

Jenny narrows her eyes, already suspicious. "What?"

Sloan smirks. "You and Callum, huh?"

Jenny scoffs, rolling her eyes. "Oh, come on. That's old news."

"I don't know... I thought I saw a little flirting happening." Sloan nudges her playfully. "Maybe this trip could rekindle some old flames." She bumps Jenny's shoulder with hers.

Jenny lifts a shoulder, feigning indifference. "Innocent flirting never hurt anybody, Sloan." Then, after a beat, she grins. "But I'm not saying no either. So... we'll see."

Back at the hotel, Jenny suggests they keep the celebration going at the bar. Callum orders a round of shots. Soon, the bartender returns with two Jameson shots and three Lemon Drops.

They all clink glasses and throw back their drinks.

Jenny feels her phone vibrate in her crossbody bag. She pulls it out—voicemail from her mom. Great. She gestures to Sloan that she's stepping away, then presses her phone to her ear as she walks toward a quieter spot.

Her mom's voice is firm the second the message plays.

"Hi, Jenny. I don't know if you forgot who I am, but I'm the woman who gave birth to you. I thought I should remind you since it seems like you're forgetting a lot these days. You forgot that I asked you to pick your dad and me up from the airport today. I've been calling nonstop—no answer. I had to sit in some strange man's car and take an Uber home, honey. Do you know how embarrassing that was? I drove by your house because I thought something might have happened. I'm sitting outside right now, no one's answering, the lights are off... something's up, and I don't like it. Call me when you get this."

Jenny's stomach twists. She hasn't had much service since arriving in the mountains, but it wouldn't matter now. There was no point in calling back. Not yet. She exhales, slipping her phone back into her bag before heading back to join the group.

When she returns, Ferris looks like he's in the middle of giving an important speech. He glances up, noticing her.

"Alright, Jenny, we were just discussing our wedding. This has to stay a secret until we announce it at the reception." His arm is wrapped around Sloan, who's grinning up at him.

Callum looks over at Jenny, winks, and then turns back to the group. "You know Jenny won't have a problem keeping a secret. This woman is *full* of secrets."

Jenny throws a glance over her shoulder, then back at Callum, touching her chest in mock innocence. "Who, me? I'm an open book." She swats his arm playfully, knowing *exactly* what he means—old memories and half-kept promises that neither of them ever fully addressed.

They hadn't been an item in years, but somehow, just like that, she's pulled right back in.

She clears her throat. "Oh, by the way, Mom called. Left a message asking where we are. So... some heat might be coming when she finds out."

Ferris doesn't even blink. "Honestly, it'd be weird if she didn't give us some heat. Last time we talked, she was still uninvited from the wedding."

The group bursts into laughter, the tension of the earlier conversation melting away. Sloan shakes her head, taking a sip of her drink. "Well, at least she's consistent."

Sloan's mom eventually excuses herself for the night, offering a tired smile before heading up to her room, but the four of them aren't ready to call it a night just yet.

They keep the celebration going—ordering another round, swapping stories, and dancing to whatever song spills through the speakers. Laughter bubbles up between them, easy and unfiltered, as if they've momentarily stepped out of time, caught up in the perfect buzz of a night well spent.

A few hours later, Ferris and Sloan exchange a look before Ferris stretches his arms over his head with a satisfied sigh. "Alright, I think we're officially in newlywed mode. We're heading up."

Jenny smirks, lifting her glass. "Go live your best married life."

As they disappear up to their room, Jenny turns back to Callum, the familiar spark between them still lingering. Their eyes meet, and for a moment, it feels like old times—before life got in the way, before things became complicated.

Chapter 25

The next morning Ferris and Sloan are sipping coffee in bed together when there's a knock on the door letting them know their room service arrived. Ferris scoots out of bed to pull in the cart and delivers Sloan's plate.

She quickly pulls off the cover and dives into her pancakes. Ferris is spreading some butter on his bread before taking a bite. "I'm starving. I feel like we barely ate yesterday."

Sloan nods in agreement as she bites down on her piece of bacon. "I'm really glad we came back to the room when we did last night. Callum had just ordered a drink when we were leaving, so I really wonder what time they went back to their rooms?"

As they talk, Sloan and Ferris share a quiet moment of contentment. There's a deep sense of relief that washes over both of them, knowing they made the right decision. They laugh about the spontaneity of it all—the rush of excitement that came with sneaking off and making it official without any of the usual fanfare. It feels so right, so freeing.

Sloan looks at Ferris, her heart swelling with happiness. "We did it, didn't we? We're really married."

Ferris smiles, his eyes softening with affection as he nods. "Yeah, and I wouldn't have had it any other way." Their shared joy is palpable, and despite the looming reception, they both know that their love for each other is the only thing that matters.

Ferris knows how much Sloan has dealt with throughout the entire wedding planning process, and he hopes this spontaneous decision shows her just how deeply in love with her he is. He's ready to prove, in every possible way, that he would do anything for her—even if that means putting a permanent wedge between himself and his mother.

Down the hall in another hotel room, Callum wakes up to a text from his neighbor. He'd only told him he was headed out of town, just to have someone keeping an eye on his place. His neighbor mentions that Gretchen is still at the apartment, so he isn't sure why Callum needed to worry about the place after all. Callum makes a few quiet grunts to show his irritation upon learning that Gretchen is still there after clearly telling her she had one night. It's now been two.

Callum decides to send Gretchen a quick text to give her a heads-up that he'll be home tonight. He tells her to make sure she and all her things are gone because he doesn't want to see her. It struck him as odd that he hadn't heard from Gretchen at all since he left—she had no idea he'd taken a spontaneous trip, so it was strange that she was still there.

After sending the text, he sits up in bed, stretches out his arms, and lets out a sigh, muttering to himself, "Ugh, I swear if she's there in my apartment when I get back, I don't know what I'm gonna do."

Just then, there's a rustle under the covers next to him, and Jenny rolls over. Her eyes are still closed, but she responds with a quiet mumble, "I'm sure it'll be fine, Cal. But really, I don't know why you trusted her to leave your house when she said she would. She's never been trustworthy." She throws her hand to her forehead as if to show she has a slight headache.

He freezes, forgetting what he told Jenny about Gretchen last night and now wondering what she just heard him mumble about the situation this morning. She stretches out, her toes brushing against his leg, and his heart skips a beat.

"I forgot how easy this used to be between us," she mumbles, then turns to look at him, her voice softer now. It felt surprisingly natural waking up next to Callum—no awkwardness. Just... familiar.

Callum meets her gaze and lets out a quiet breath, the corners of his mouth lifting slightly. "Yeah... this is really nice." He says it like he means it—like it surprises him how much it does.

But then his expression shifts, the weight of the other thing still tugging at him. "You're right about Gretchen. She's never really been trustworthy." He turns, running a hand through his hair.

"I left in a hurry, and with the trip and everything, I just wasn't thinking. I just have this weird gut feeling that she did something."

Jenny shifts, fully opening her eyes as she sits up. She spots her clothes still on the floor and quickly pulls the covers up to her neck before smirking at him. "I know you guys just broke up and all, but I can't think of anything less sexy than being in bed with a guy while he talks about his ex," she says, grabbing her water off the nightstand and taking a big gulp. "Can we leave all that at home until we're at least back at the airport?"

Callum looks like he's going to respond, but instead, he mouths "sorry" and slides in closer to her.

She sets her water down and tilts her head. "Look, if you want, when we land tonight, I'll go back to your place with you, and we can scope it out."

And just like that, it was almost like Jenny had been under hypnosis. *Airport* was her trigger word. She instantly remembered—her mom had left her a voicemail last night. "Oh my gosh, I have to call my mom back," she says as she quickly grabs her clothes from the floor and runs into the bathroom.

"Oh, hi, Jenny," her mom quickly picks up the phone, unamused. "You better be calling me from the grave or the hospital to take that long to call me back.

"Hi, Mom. Lovely to hear your voice," Jenny sarcastically replies while shuffling around the bathroom and throwing sweatpants on. She notices how messy the bathroom is and starts trying to straighten up forgetting she's on the phone.

"Well, I'm waiting," Kate's frustration is blatant. "What's going on? Why are you taking so long to call me back?" She's standing at the front of her house looking at her front window with her hand on her hip.

"Because, Mom, I have a life that doesn't revolve around answering your phone calls 24-7. I've been busy helping with the wedding, catching up on school work, and working." Jenny takes a look in the bathroom mirror noticing she still has makeup left around her eyes.

Kate isn't buying any of it. Jenny explains that she had a headache and forgot to pick her up. This would be an okay explanation for many people, but not Kate.

"You know, this is really disappointing. Everything I do for you kids and I don't even get a phone call back. Speaking of, have you talked to your brother? I sent him and Sloan a nice fruit basket and neither of them had the decency to say 'thank you'." She feels hot in her face and takes a deep breath, remembering how mad she is.

Jenny is really getting sick of coming up with excuses these days. "You know what, I don't know if this is shocking to you, but I'm not Ferris's keeper." She tells Kate she talked to Ferris the other day and reminds her that a fruit basket won't fix all the damage she's caused these last few months.

With that, Kate huffs and mumbles, "So ungrateful. I've got to go, Jenny. If you hear from your brother, you tell him I need him to call me back." And with that, she hangs up the phone.

Later that afternoon, the five of them are packed and heading to the airport, running on caffeine and adrenaline from everything that just happened. Ferris and Sloan are still soaking in the reality of being married, happy with their decision, but unsure of how to navigate what's to inevitably come. Jenny and Callum, on the other hand, are left with a different kind of uncertainty.

They land back in Milwaukee, and all go their separate ways. Well, sort of. Ferris and Sloan go to their house, and Sloan's mom goes to hers, but Jenny hops in the car with Callum to head to his.

When Ferris and Sloan pull up to their house, they notice a fruit basket sitting on their front porch with a note. A faint sour scent lingers in the warm air, hinting at the overripe bananas that have started to brown and soften. Grapes, once plump and taut, now sag on their stems, some beginning to shrivel. The pears have taken on a waxy sheen, their skin showing the first signs of wrinkling. A few gnats hover nearby, drawn to the sticky spots where juice has leaked from a punctured peach. The basket, meant to be a gesture of kindness, now looks more like an afterthought, forgotten and slowly surrendering to time.

Ferris notices a card on the front and pulls it off and begins to open it.

"Who's it from?" Sloan curiously asks.

Annoyance washes over Ferris's face. "It's from my mom." And with that, he picks up the entire fruit basket, walks over to their garbage, and tosses it in. He walks back to Sloan, grabs their luggage, and begins to walk into the house. "Now, where were we?"

***

On the other side of town, Callum and Jenny pull up at his place. He doesn't see Gretchen's car, so that seems like a good sign.

They get out of the car together and walk up to his apartment door. Callum pulls the keys out of his pocket and opens it up. He walks in first through the living room keeping a close eye to try to not miss any detail. Jenny follows behind a few steps.

"Look Callum, I don't know what you were worried about. Your place looks perfectly fine," Jenny is standing in the hall looking around the place when she turns to see Callum with a blank stare on his face peering into his room.

She slowly steps into his room and takes it all in—the TV ripped off the wall, the bed completely gone, deep scratches gouged into the dresser, and the bathroom mirror shattered.

"Oh, that's bad," Jenny mutters, walking up behind Callum, who's still standing there, trying to process what he's seeing.

He starts to walk into the closet and begins frantically pushing through clothes and boxes. "My suit and shoes for the wedding. I just had that tailored. They're completely gone. Everything for the wedding is gone. She's trying to destroy me." He throws his head back and combs his fingers back through his hair. "I knew it."

Jenny stands there uncomfortably and looks over at Callum, who is clearly defeated. "Is it too late to say I think you should change the locks?"

Chapter 26

Callum hangs up the phone with the police. Now phase two of the plan to get his stuff back is in motion. He paces his apartment nervously while Jenny snaps photos of the damage in his room. She walks over, gives him a reassuring pat on the back, and flashes a thumbs-up.

He exhales sharply and dials. As the phone rings, his hopeful expression quickly falters. "It's going to voicemail." He clears his throat and leaves a message.

"Hey, Gretchen, it's Callum. Look, I just feel terrible about how things ended, and I really want to make it up to you. I should have never acted so rashly. You and Christy mean so much to me, and I was just overwhelmed. I really think we belong together, so please, give me a call back. I hope we can fix this."

He hangs up and glances at Jenny, who's casually pouring herself a cup of coffee. "You really think this will work?"

Jenny smirks, all confidence. "Oh yeah. She's clinging to you like a life raft at this point. She'll come crawling back." She opens the fridge for creamer, comes up empty, and sighs before settling at the table to wait for the trap to spring.

Minutes later, Callum's phone buzzes. Gretchen. He answers quickly, masking his disgust with warmth.

"I just got your message," Gretchen says, her tone syrupy. "Look, I'm so sorry too. I'd love a chance to sit down and talk—make things right."

Callum plays along. "Yeah, I would too. I'm at my place now."

Before he can say more, Gretchen jumps in. "Okay, but... before you go into your room, I have to tell you something. I, um, took your bed." She exhales dramatically. "You left me no choice, Callum! My parents' house didn't even have one for me."

Callum grits his teeth but keeps his voice even. "Oh, I get it." he pauses pretending to walk into his room to notice the TV. "And you needed my TV?"

"The TV was... well, I was mad, okay?" she continues. "I wanted you to feel the pain of losing me."

He knows she's full of it, but the goal is to get her back over here. "I totally get it. Why don't you come over now so we can talk through everything?"

Gretchen takes the bait. "Really? You mean it?"

"Of course," he says smoothly. Then, as if it's an afterthought, he adds, "Oh, and before you leave—looks like my suit for the wedding is missing too. Maybe bring that over, and we can try on our wedding clothes together?"

"Well, I'm still not going to that wedding for those awful friends of yours," Gretchen says.

"Of course not. There's no way I'm going either, but if you don't bring those clothes back over, how will I take you on the romantic date I have planned for us?"

Jenny, watching from across the room, groans and rolls her eyes so hard they might get stuck. Callum shrugs helplessly.

Gretchen excitedly agrees and hangs up. As soon as the call ends, Callum dials the police. "She's on her way."

Fifteen minutes later, a car door slams outside. Jenny darts to the blinds, peeks out, and sprints back to the kitchen to hide. "The Devil is here! I mean, Gretchen."

Callum takes a steadying breath before opening the door. He greets Gretchen with a forced hug. She nervously holds up his suit like a peace offering. "Here it is! Your suit!" she says brightly like she didn't steal it in the first place. "Just the way you left it."

Callum takes it, nodding. "Appreciate it."

She smiles, twirling a strand of hair around her finger. "I obviously couldn't carry the bed and TV over, but we can bring them later... you know, when the time is right." She steps inside, already kicking off her shoes.

Callum blocks her path. "Thanks for the suit, but yeah, I won't be asking you to stay."

Gretchen freezes, her wide eyes scanning the room like she's being Punk'd. "What are you talking about? I thought you wanted to work things out?" She tries to move past him, but he stands firm.

"You stole thousands of dollars worth of stuff from me and trashed my apartment, Gretchen. And honestly? Even if you hadn't done all that, you're just a terrible person. There's no way in hell I'd ever get back with you."

Gretchen shrieks, her composure shattering. "UGH! I should have known you were lying! God, you're such a loser." She whirls around—and stops dead when she sees Jenny stepping out of the kitchen.

"What's she doing here?" Gretchen's face twists with rage. She lunges, shoving Callum aside and reaching for Jenny's hair.

Before she makes contact, there's a loud bang on the door.

Callum doesn't hesitate. "Come in!"

Two police officers stride in, just as Gretchen swings for Jenny.

"Hands off!" one officer barks. "Gretchen Bialt, you are under arrest for theft of private property and vandalizing a residence. And if you keep going, you're looking at an additional charge for assault and battery."

Gretchen's hands fly up. "What? No! I didn't steal anything—I live here!"

One of the officers pulls out a pair of handcuffs. "Sorry, ma'am, your name's not on the lease. These items aren't yours. We have all the proof we need."

Gretchen tries to back away, panic setting in. "This has to be a joke. I cannot get arrested. And why is she even here?!" She jerks her head toward Jenny.

"Miss, we are not playing around," the officer warns. "If you resist again, you're going to have bigger problems." He grabs her arm, cuffs her, and starts guiding her toward the door.

Gretchen twists to glare at Jenny and Callum, her face dark with fury, like she's already plotting revenge.

As soon as she's out the door, Jenny and Callum exhale in unison.

Callum glances at the suit in his hands and shakes his head. "Well, I'm still without a bed, but at least I got my suit back?"

Jenny laughs, linking her arm through his. "Come on. I think I've got an extra spot in my bed."

Chapter 27

It's now the week before the wedding reception. Sloan is busy reviewing the timeline while Ferris makes final calls to vendors. Just as he sits down at the kitchen table, his phone buzzes. He glances at the screen, hesitates, then answers. "Hey, Dad."

His father's voice was soft, almost hesitant. "Hey, son. I just... wanted to check-in. I'm sorry to put another thing on your plate, but your mom's been crying off and on all week. She's having a hard time coming to terms with missing your special day."

A pause.

"I respect your decision, of course. But I don't want you to look back and regret not having her there. I know she can be difficult... but she means well. She's just never known how to show it."

Ferris rubs his forehead, letting the silence settle for a second. "I hear you, but I've made my decision." he pauses, realizing he was maybe harsh, "I'll think about it." He softens his tone. "Thanks for calling, Dad, but we've gotta finish some stuff for the wedding."

"Of course. I love you, kid."

"Love you too."

He hangs up, the weight of it all pressing down on him. The room was quiet—too quiet.

Sloan looked up from the couch with concern in her eyes. She didn't have to ask. She could already see it.

***

Later that evening Ferris and Sloan are finalizing the seating arrangements for the wedding reception. Sloan is sitting on the floor with a poster board and moving around sticky notes with guests' names on them as Ferris stands behind her overhead.

Each table looks appropriately filled when they get to Ferris's immediate family table. Sloan picks up the sticky note with his mom's name and holds it in her hand. She looks up at Ferris, confused about what to do next. She then picks up Ferris's dad's and moves it around like she's playing her next move in chess.

Suddenly the table looks empty. Now that table would only have an aunt, two cousins, and grandma. Ferris wasn't even certain his dad would show up without his mom.

Sloan puts both sticky notes down and looks back up at Ferris. "Look, I can't do this. Your family should be there at our reception."

Ferris puts his hand up, "No, I know you feel like you have to please everyone around you, but I want you to feel like a queen."

Sloan stands up next to Ferris, puts her arms on his shoulders, and turns his body towards hers. "I know you are protecting me, and I appreciate it. But if we don't invite your mom, where does that leave your dad? He did nothing to deserve this, and he'll be put in a very awkward position. I don't want to even risk that he doesn't show up. One of us needs to have our dad there," she slides her hands down his arms so she's holding his hands. "And if you're concerned that I won't feel like a queen, you're mistaken. I'm already with you. You're my king. Nothing that happens will take away how I feel about you." Sloan's eyes well up with tears.

Ferris moves his hand up to graze her jawline. "You're truly amazing, you know that? I know your dad is looking down on you, proud as ever."

Sloan wipes away a tear. "I wish you could have met him. I know I always say it, but he would have loved you." And just like that, without having to say anything she leans into Ferris. He pulls her in and wraps his arms around her tightly.

They decide together to re-invite his mom to the wedding reception—not because they forgive her, but because they don't want to put his dad in a difficult position and cause him more stress. Ferris's table should be just as full with family. After sleeping on it, they call Kate the next morning. She's quiet on the phone, suspicion lingering, but her excitement is unmistakable.

***

The wedding day is finally here. Jenny and Sloan are in the bridal suite with Sloan's mom and the other bridesmaids getting ready for the wedding. Jenny, wearing her navy-blue silk pajamas and hair in a half-up-do and curls, is running around the room making sure everything is taken care of.

Sloan sits in the chair getting the final touches to her hair. She's wearing her white silk bridal pajamas and the hairstylist is keeping her hair simple, yet elegant with loose curls and a thin bridal tiara. Her mom stands over to the side sipping her champagne beaming watching her daughter get pampered.

Just then, the photographer arrives, and Jenny greets them at the door and gestures to them to come in. They set up their things and start snapping candid photos around the room.

The day-of-coordinator, Ivette, pops in after setting up the venue downstairs and indicates she would like to do a quick run-through of the timeline for the wedding since things have changed and she wants to ensure no mixups.

Jenny quickly grabs her tablet and takes a seat next to Ivette. "Okay, so Sloan and I figured out the plan last night. When everyone starts to arrive, they're going to be invited to grab a drink at the bar. Then, at three-fifteen, the DJ will announce that everyone needs to take their seats. We will line up like normal, bridesmaids with groomsmen, myself with the best man, Callum, then a long pause, and Ferris and Sloan will walk out together."

Ivette looks confused as she's making a note. "Together?"

Sloan sits up from her chair and confirms, "Yes, together. Ferris and I prepared a little speech to basically announce we already got married."

Ivette stops and opens her eyes wide, looking at Sloan and then back at Jenny. "Well, I thought I had seen it all, but I've never seen this before. I'm excited!" She quickly jots down a note, then tells them she's off to check on the guys and that they've got another hour before it's time to get dressed and head downstairs.

A little while later Sloan is sitting calmly, eyes closed as the makeup artist dusts highlighter across her cheekbones. Jenny, now in the chair next to her, is getting the final touches on her lips—the last step before she can help Sloan into her dress. The morning has been nothing short of perfect—relaxing, filled with laughter, and just the right amount of excited nerves. Exactly how they had planned it.

Soft music plays in the background, the scent of fresh peonies filling the suite. Everything feels peaceful. Effortless.

And then—click, click, click. The sharp staccato of heels echoes down the hallway, breaking through the serene atmosphere like a warning shot.

A familiar voice follows, sing-song and unmistakably proud. "Happy Wedding Day! Mother of the Groom here!"

All heads turn toward the door just as Kate sweeps in. Her brown hair is now highlighted with blonde streaks and is teased higher than usual, stiff with hairspray. Her signature bright pink blush is extra heavy today, nearly neon against her cheekbones. But none of that is what makes the room fall into stunned silence.

It's her dress.

Floor-length. Glittering. And *white.*

Sloan's stomach knots so hard she feels sick. Jenny makes a strangled noise, somewhere between a gasp and a choke. Even the makeup artist—who is literally paid to stay neutral—lets out a barely concealed "Oh."

Kate beams, smoothing her hands down the sequined fabric, completely oblivious to the horror she's just unleashed. "What do you guys think? Don't I look amazing? Because I sure feel it!" She notices everyone staring at her, jaws slack, but takes it as a compliment. "You're all speechless, yes! That's exactly what I was going for."

She glides toward the breakfast bar, grabbing the open bottle of champagne. "Anyways, who wants champagne?" Before anyone can answer, she pours a glass and practically thrusts it at Sloan, winking. "Champagne for the bride?"

Sloan, eyes closed as the makeup artist applies her fake lashes, doesn't even look at her. "No, thank you. I already have a glass. And I don't want to mess up my lipstick." She wants to say something but is trying her best to remain relaxed and focus on what's ahead.

Jenny, still staring in pure disbelief, suddenly finds her voice. "Mom, what the HELL are you wearing?"

Kate blinks at her like she just asked what color the sky was. "I'm wearing a custom Vera Wang evening gown." She preens. "My son's wedding only deserves the best."

Jenny throws up her hands. "MOM. IT'S WHITE."

Kate waves a dismissive hand, already spinning toward the floor-length mirror to admire herself. "Jenny, it's cream. You need to get your eyes checked." She plucks the untouched flute of champagne from the table near Sloan and shoves it at Jenny instead. "Here, I think you need this."

Then, as if this whole thing is just business as usual, Kate glances at her phone. "Well, would you look at that? It's about time for my moment." She tosses her hair, smiling at her reflection like a villain in a soap opera. "I'm off to find Ferris so he can escort me down the aisle. Bye!" She quickly shuffles out of the room, but not before giving an airy, forceful hug to Sloan's mom as she walks out of the bathroom.

"So, she's always completely clueless, huh?" Virginia walks over to Sloan.

Sloan shakes her head profusely, "Well she's in for a big surprise when she realizes she's not walking Ferris down the aisle."

Jenny laughs, "I think that surprise is the least of her worries."

Chapter 28

Ferris, Callum, and his two other groomsmen lounge in the hotel room, casually throwing back beers while they wait for the signal to head downstairs. The mood is light, filled with laughter and easy conversation.

Then—knock, knock.

Before anyone can react, the door swings open.

"Hey, boys!"

Kate sweeps into the room, her energy as grand as the entrance itself. Ferris nearly chokes on his drink. Callum, mid-laugh, stops short. His other friends exchange looks.

"Oh, my darling!" Kate beams, immediately gravitating toward Ferris, cupping his face in her hands.

"Oh, hey, Mom," he mumbles, already bracing himself.

She pulls back, eyes raking over him approvingly. "Ugh, you just pull off this look so well." She winks. "But anyway, honey, it's about that time. Let's lock up our arms and walk down that aisle."

Ferris blinks. "What?"

Kate frowns. "What do you mean, 'what'? We're walking down together."

He rubs the back of his neck. "Mom... no, we're not."

Her smile falters. "I'm sorry—what do you mean?" Her voice tightens, her hands gesturing to herself. "Why do you think I got dressed like this?"

Ferris finally takes in her outfit. The sequins. The floor-length gown. The very, very *white* floor-length gown.

Callum lets out a low whistle. "Uh... is that... white?"

Kate's head snaps toward him. "No! Gosh, why is everyone saying that?" She waves a dismissive hand. "It's *off-white. Cream.* Perfectly acceptable, okay?"

Ferris exhales slowly. "Mom, Sloan and I are doing a first look in a few minutes, and then *we* are walking down the aisle together."

Kate blinks. Once. Twice. Then, she tilts her head, eyes narrowing. "Walk down together?" She lets out a dry laugh. "What kind of modern bullshit is this?"

Ferris's jaw tightens. "Mom, I'm only going to say this once. You're *lucky* you were re-invited to this wedding. This is your chance to prove that you're here to support us. Go change, I will not have you wearing that."

The room goes still. Even Callum, usually the first to crack a joke, takes a slow sip of his beer instead.

Kate stares at him, speechless for once.

Ferris steps closer, voice low, sharp. "So, here's how this is going to go—you're going to accept what we say and follow our lead. Otherwise, security will be *more than happy* to escort you out."

A beat.

Kate sighs, unfazed, pulling out her lipstick and reapplying it with a dramatic swipe. "Fine." She waves a hand. "Where's your father?"

Ferris checks his watch. "Last I saw, he was heading back to your hotel room. Said he was looking for a belt."

Kate scoffs. "Of course, he was. Well, I guess I'll walk down with him then." She spins on her heel, already halfway to the door. "Bye, boys."

The door clicks shut behind her.

Silence.

Then, Callum lets out a low laugh, shaking his head. "Man, your mom is *wild*."

Ferris lets out a long breath. "You have no idea."

Chapter 29

The room hums with quiet excitement as Jenny and their mother fuss over the final touches of Sloan's gown. An off-the-shoulder, backless A-line dress—timeless, effortless, and perfectly her.

The silky fabric pools around her feet as Jenny smooths out an invisible wrinkle, stepping back to admire her work. "Okay," she exhales, her hands on her hips. "Moment of truth."

Sloan turns to the full-length mirror. For a second, she barely recognizes herself. Not because of the dress or the elegant way her hair is styled, but because of the way she feels—weightless, glowing, ready.

Behind her, Virginia presses a hand to her heart, her eyes already shimmering with unshed tears. "Oh, honey," she breathes. "You look—" She stops, shaking her head with a watery smile. "Your dad would be so proud of you."

Sloan's chest tightens, but it's a good ache. She meets her mom's gaze in the mirror, and for a moment, it's just them. "I know," she whispers, her voice steady despite the lump in her throat. "I feel it."

Her mom squeezes her shoulders gently, and Sloan leans into the touch, allowing herself this one quiet moment before the day sweeps her away.

Jenny claps her hands together, sniffling. "Okay, enough, I'm about to ruin my mascara." She takes Sloan's hands, squeezing tight. "Are you ready for this?"

Sloan breathes in. Breathes out.

***

Minutes pass, but they barely register. The air in the bridal suite is charged—excitement, nerves, love. All of it swirling together.

Sloan smooths her dress for what feels like the millionth time, her fingers trembling. Not from nerves. From something bigger. The weight of it all—the day, the people, the expectations—presses in from every angle. But none of it matters. None of it ever matters when it's just them.

Across the hall, Ferris lets out a slow breath, rolling his shoulders like he's trying to shake off the day's chaos. He's already won. The moment they signed their marriage license, the moment she became his wife, he had everything he ever needed. But this? This moment is for them.

They insisted on it. Not because they needed to follow a timeline, but because they needed each other—a quiet moment to breathe, to hold on to what this day is really about. Before the speeches, the dancing, the noise. Before the eyes of a hundred people who love them.

A door creaks open.

Sloan steps into the hallway, her heart hammering, breath catching the second she sees him.

Ferris turns.

And just like that, the world shrinks down to only them.

His expression shifts—awe, reverence, something deeper than words. His eyes sweep over her like he's memorizing her all over again. Like he'd marry her a thousand times over if she'd let him.

Sloan exhales, her lips parting, but no words come. There's nothing to say. She steps forward, and in an instant, Ferris is there, wrapping her in his arms and pressing his forehead to hers.

Everything else fades. The chaos, the expectations, even the whispers from down the hall.

This is what matters.

Them. Together. Two parts of a whole, stepping into this next chapter, side by side.

Ferris tilts her chin up, his thumb grazing her cheek. "You ready?"

Sloan smiles, her hands tightening around his. "Always."

***

"Ugh, Ted, you took too long finding your belt. I'm going to miss my grand entrance!" Kate huffs, arm looped around her husband's as she drags him down the wedding hall, cutting through the seats, still wearing her white gown. "We need the front row for our family."

As they near the front, she notices Virginia sitting front and center. She stops to the side of her, hands on her hips. "Ahem, you're in my seat. I'm going to need you to move over."

Virginia, unbothered, barely looks up. "I'm sorry, I didn't see your name on this seat. But this seemed like the best one for getting the best view of my daughter and son-in-law."

Kate's lips tighten. "Okay, but this one has a better view of my son."

Virginia doesn't flinch. She simply smiles a little too wide, turns slowly, and meets Kate's gaze. "Kate, I hate to tell you this, but I was told to keep an eye on you. Any funny business, and you're out of here. So, what do you think? Would you like to sit over there, or should I suggest somewhere across the street?" She gestures to the other side of the aisle.

Kate's face tightens, but she nods stiffly and heads to the other side with Ted, her pride only slightly bruised.

Ivette is bustling around, organizing the wedding party and getting everyone in their places. Jenny and Callum stand side by side, looking at each other with an easy smile.

Jenny reaches up, straightening Callum's tie. "You clean up nice."

Callum grins, tousling her hair as he loops his arm in hers. "Could say the same for you."

Ivette gives a nod to the DJ, who starts off with soft, elegant music for the wedding party's entrance. It teases the crowd, building anticipation as the guests settle in. But without warning, the music shifts dramatically to "I Believe in a Thing Called Love" by The Darkness.

Ivette's eyes widen in surprise, but she leans in and whispers, "Alright, go ahead, guys."

Kate's eyes narrow, her expression hardening as confusion twists across her face. She doesn't yell or flail—she simply stands frozen, her posture stiff, hands clenched tightly in front of her. Her jaw tightens as she watches the DJ nod along with the music, clearly unbothered.

Ferris and Sloan are already gliding down the aisle, hands clasped, their smiles wide and genuine as they sing along to one of their favorite songs, completely carefree and in their element.

When Ferris and Sloan get to the altar in front of everyone, the music stops and Kate slowly sits back in her seat, curious about what is happening. Ferris picks up the microphone and holds it in front of the both of them, "Hi everyone, we just wanna thank you so much for coming here and celebrating with us. It means everything."

Sloan jumps in, "If you are here in this room, it's because you've supported us, loved us, or just helped us along the way in our journey." She looks down, directly at her mom.

Ferris continues, "And I know you all came today expecting to witness a beautiful ceremony between Sloan and myself. However, we weren't completely honest about one thing."

Kate, who had placed her hand over her heart in dramatic expectation, suddenly pulls it away, gripping her legs tightly instead, holding on for safety.

Ferris subtly grabs Sloan's hand, "We have some very exciting news to share, and it might seem a little shocking at first, but we can get to the party a little bit quicker because," he pauses to look at Sloan like he's about to burst, "Sloan and I actually decided to follow our hearts and get married spontaneously at the Grand Canyon a few weeks ago. So, we are here to celebrate in a big party style, with all of you guys as witnesses into the next chapter of our lives!"

Kate leaps off her chair and steps out into the aisle, saying, "What?" but no one can hear her over the excitement and cheers from the crowd.

Sloan notices Kate's fury building—like she's one second away from hopping onto the altar and grabbing the microphone—so she starts speaking louder and quicker.

"And we just can't wait to celebrate with you all tonight! The bar is open, the DJ's ready to play, and dinner will be served shortly. Please enjoy yourselves—and let's make the most of today!"

The DJ queues up Blink 182's *"First Date,"* another one of their favorites. Ferris gently pulls the microphone down from her face, winks, and together, they run hand-in-hand back down the aisle.

"Sloan, Ferris, I demand to know what's going on here!" Kate yells, trying to storm after them. But they don't even glance her way—they're too busy laughing, celebrating, and soaking in the moment. Frustrated, Kate stops in her tracks and whirls around, locking eyes with Virginia on the other side of the aisle.

"Did you know about this? Why don't you look as surprised as everybody else here?"

Virginia stands up, proudly, "Because I was there when they exchanged vows. Did you miss your invite?" she pauses with a sarcastic glare, "Or, oh, maybe you didn't get one."

Kate throws her hands up, "What? This is ridiculous! Ted! Did you know about this?"

Ted, looking confused as ever, is looking around to see where Ferris and Sloan ran off to. "What? No, I didn't know this was happening."

***

Ferris and Sloan find themselves alone for a brief moment after the ceremony—tucked just out of view behind the floral archway. The music fades slightly, the noise of the crowd drifting into the background.

Sloan wraps her arms around his waist, and he holds her close, pressing a kiss to the top of her head. "I love you," she murmurs into his chest. "We did this. Not despite everything, but because of everything. Thanks for choosing me."

Ferris pulls back just enough to meet her eyes. "I love you more."

For the first time all day, the tension melts from their shoulders. They pull apart with a shared smile and begin walking toward the bar, where Jenny and Callum are already waiting—drinks in hand and grins ready.

Chapter 30

"I need to talk to my son." Kate pushes through the crowd of people who are enjoying themselves getting drinks and dancing. She makes her way up to the bar where Ferris and Sloan are standing with Jenny and Callum. "Ferris, I demand to know what's going on right now."

Ferris doesn't turn, he's looking at Sloan, making a clear divide.

"Ferris!" She yells out again.

While still looking at Sloan, Ferris lifts his hand to gently tousle a piece of her hair, his fingers trailing along her jawline as he says, "I'm sorry, I'm a little busy enjoying my wedding day right now. If you aren't here to enjoy the day and support my wife and I, then you can see your way out."

Sloan had never been more in love with Ferris than in that moment.

HERE COMES THE DRAMA

And just then, as Jenny turns to give Ferris a comforting smile, someone bumps into her from behind. The impact sends her stumbling forward—right into a guest holding a full glass of red wine, which splashes all over Kate's pristine, off-white dress.

Kate freezes, her jaw hanging open in shock. For a moment, there's silence, everyone staring at what just happened.

"Are you kidding me?" Kate screeches, as the red stain spreads across her dress like wildfire. "This is the most humiliating day of my life!"

Sloan turns into Ferris's arms and, with a smirk, says, "Well, at least now you'll match the wedding color."

Kate, in her wine-soaked fury, glares at everyone, her face beet-red as she storms off. As she walks away, the last thing anyone hears is her yelling, "You'll regret this!"

Ferris pulls Sloan in close, pressing a kiss to her forehead as they watch Kate storm off. Sloan sighs happily. "Well, there goes the drama."

Ferris smirks, lacing his fingers through hers. "And here's to our next chapter—hopefully drama-free."

Sloan glances up at him, her voice barely above a whisper. "Do you think it's really over?"

Ferris squeezes her hand, the corner of his mouth lifting in a quiet, tired smile. "She's always going to be who she is." He pauses, then adds with certainty, "But now? That's not our problem."

A Letter To Sloan

It's the morning after our wedding—well, the wedding reception.

I woke up to the warmth of Ferris next to me and sunlight pouring through the window. I rolled toward him and pressed a soft kiss to his shoulder. He didn't open his eyes, but he smiled, and in that moment, everything felt exactly as it should be.

This is it. My future.

For a second, I just laid there—eyes closed, heart full—and let it all sink in.

It's all behind us now.

The chaos. The noise. The drama.

We made it through, and somehow… we're stronger for it. I feel grounded. I feel seen. I feel loved in a way I didn't know I could be.

And for the first time in a long time, I'm not bracing for what comes next.

I'm excited.

For quiet mornings. For new memories. For all the things we get to build from here.

We're on the other side now.
And it's beautiful here.

Love,
Sloan

BONUS SCENE

Just Married

The late afternoon sun spills across the private deck, casting a golden haze over the edge of the infinity pool. Sloan leans back in a lounge chair, her legs stretched out, sunglasses slipping slightly down her nose.

Suddenly, Ferris emerges from the villa with sunglasses perched on his head, wearing black swim trunks and holding two glasses of champagne.

"My beautiful wife, the champagne you ordered," Ferris says with a wink, leaning forward to hand one to Sloan.

She laughs and sits up, reaching for the glass. "I could get used to this. The sun, the fresh air, no drama." She gestures up to the sky as if to thank the sun directly.

Ferris gently settles into the lounge chair beside her and takes a deep breath, soaking it all in.

She turns to face him and lifts her glass to clink his. "To married life. I'm so ready for this next chapter." She leans in to give him a quick peck on the cheek.

"To married life," Ferris echoes, smirking at her before taking a long sip. He lets out an audible, satisfied *ahh* before adding, "Tell you what, if I could just sit at a resort like this with you by my side and a drink in my hand for the rest of my life, I think I could die happy."

Sloan, now reclining again, mumbles, "You sure we didn't actually die from the wedding stress and this is heaven?" She laughs.

Ferris chuckles. "Come to think of it, the end was kind of a blur... an out-of-body experience." He thinks back to the moment he made a clear divide between his new wife and his mother, proud of the way he stood his ground—hoping Sloan never second-guesses where she stands again.

He glances over at her, admiring how she glows so naturally in the sunlight. He can hardly keep his hands off her. Setting down his champagne glass, he moves to sit on her chair, gently cups her face, and leans in for a soft kiss.

She lifts her head to meet him, kissing him back, her hands exploring his warm body. He slides fully onto the lounge chair, silently praying it's strong enough to hold them both. His fingers trail from her collarbone down to the curves of her body—

Then there's a knock at the door.

They pause, looking at each other, then toward the villa. Without saying a word, they silently agree to ignore it and return to where they left off.

Ferris reaches for the string on Sloan's swimsuit top—

Another knock. Louder this time.

He sits up, annoyed. "Next time I'm putting the 'Do Not Disturb' sign on our door." He walks to the door and peers through the peephole. A bellhop stands there, holding something.

Ferris opens the door. The bellhop smiles, holding out a card. "For the newlyweds. A little spa treatment."

Ferris hesitates before taking the card. "Oh, um... thank you. Who's it from?"

"The caller was anonymous," the bellhop says, his smile a little too practiced. "They just said they wanted to send you a little treat before you head home."

Ferris furrows his brow. "Thanks," he repeats, watching as the bellhop walks away. He stands there for a beat, peering around the front of the villa. Nothing. Eventually, he shakes it off and heads back inside, shutting the door behind him.

"Who was that?" Sloan asks as Ferris returns to the deck.

Ferris opens the envelope and scans the card.

"Here's to making sure you relax on your honeymoon. Something tells me you're going to need it."

His stomach tightens. The words could be innocent... or something else entirely. He slides the card into his pocket and forces a smile. "Just a little spa surprise," he says. "Let's not waste it."

Acknowledgments

I would like to extend my deepest gratitude to my developmental editor and literary representation, **Jessica Berg** from **Rosecliff Literary**, for her invaluable feedback, guidance, and unwavering excitement throughout the entire process. Your expertise and encouragement were instrumental in bringing this book to life.

A special thank you to my book cover designer and dear friend, **Kasey Corona** from **Oak&Air**, for your constant support and your brilliant creation of a beautiful cover. You took my vision and transformed it into something far better than I ever could have imagined.

Authors Note

What started as a little skit on social media turned into something so much bigger than I ever imagined. Ferris and Sloan were just a funny idea I shared one day—but thanks to you, the story grew into a 16-part series and now, this book.

I'm beyond grateful to everyone who watched, commented, shared, and encouraged me to keep going. Your messages, support, and requests for "just one more episode" truly inspired me to bring this story to life on the page.

While this story is fictional, I know so many of you saw yourselves in it—because when I shared, you shared too. And through that, it became clear: behind all the chaos, drama, and laughs, there's something deeply human about navigating love, boundaries, and relationships.

Thank you for being part of this journey with me. This is just the beginning.

Until next time...
Christa

About the Author

Christa Innis is a writer, creator, and host of the *Here Comes the Drama* podcast, where she shares wild wedding stories, hot takes, and follower confessions while exploring the importance of setting boundaries. What started as a fun outlet—sharing drama-filled stories online—quickly turned into viral skits, a thriving community, and nearly 1 million followers across platforms. Now, she's thrilled to be following one of her biggest dreams—bringing her stories to life on the page.

Loved this Book?

Please leave a review—it helps more readers discover *Ferris & Sloan* and truly means the world to me.

Want to help spread the word? Tag @PartyPlanningbyChrista on TikTok, Instagram, Facebook, or YouTube for a chance to be featured or shared!

The Story's Not Over...

and there are many more to tell.

Join my newsletter or follow along on social media to stay in the loop about more content, future Ferris & Sloan updates, and more!

Visit: ChristaInnis.com/book

TikTok | Instagram | YouTube | Facebook: @PartyPlanningbyChrista

Printed in Dunstable, United Kingdom

63492151R00139